THE TEMPLE WITHIN

To my mother,
who introduced me to the Rosary

Helen Gallivan

The Temple Within

THE ROSARY, THE BIBLE
AND THE INNER JOURNEY

the columba press

First published in 2001 by
the columba press
55A Spruce Avenue, Stillorgan Industrial Park,
Blackrock, Co Dublin

Cover by Bill Bolger
Origination by The Columba Press
Printed in Ireland by ColourBooks Ltd, Dublin

ISBN 1 85607 334 3

All royalties for this book will go to
Children in Hospital Ireland.

Contents

Historical Note

Paul VI described the Rosary as the prayer of 'the simple, the poor, the illiterate and blind'. While these remarks were made in a particular context (in which change was being proposed to the form of the Rosary) and while, in an apostolic letter *Marialis Cultus*, he went on to speak of the powerful contemplative nature of the Rosary, the perception remains among many that the Rosary is an outmoded formulaic prayer, mechanical in its meaningless repetition.

The Rosary did indeed originate among the poor and the illiterate. By the fourth century AD, the recitation of the Psalter (at first daily, and later divided over a longer period) was a feature of monastic life. It was one of the principal forms of Christian prayer, inherited from the apostles and in use for twelve centuries before Christ. However, the lay brothers, being illiterate, could not recite the 150 psalms with the choir monks and the need was increasingly felt for a prayer that they could easily remember. So began the practice of reciting the Our Father 150 times, assisted by beads known as paternosters. The prayer was also adopted beyond the monasteries by unlettered people anxious to participate in some way in the liturgical life of the church.

Over time, the Lord's Prayer was supplemented by recitations of the first part of the 'Hail Mary', taken directly from scripture in the salutations to Mary by Gabriel and Elizabeth. In the thirteenth century St Dominic, often and inaccurately credited with originating the Rosary, greatly increased the spread of devotion to 'Our Lady's Psalter' as he vigorously preached its use as a weapon to combat the Albigensian heresy.

In the fifteenth century, the Gloria was added. By the sixteenth century, the second part of the 'Hail Mary' had been introduced, appearing for the first time in the Roman Breviary of 1568. This contains the title 'Mother of God' which was subsequently to be a very contentious one for the Reformed churches – who regarded it as contributing to mariolatry. The title itself dates back to the Council of Ephesus in AD 431, but some see it as no coincidence that this addition to the 'Hail Mary' should be introduced at the height of the Counter-Reformation. However, this is to ignore the fact that the early Reformers retained considerable devotion to Our Lady. Indeed, evangelist theologian and church historian David F Wright describes how the phrase 'Mother of God' remained an habitual usage for Luther throughout his life, while Zwingli 'also endorsed it explicitly'.[1] Even Calvin was less extreme in his anti-marianism than were his successors.

In that same century, Christians saw the Rosary as having contributed in a major way to victory over the Turks. It was five centuries since the first Crusade had taken place. Constantinople - bastion of Christianity - had fallen to the Turks in 1453; by 1571 they were firmly installed in many parts of Europe, while their fleets ravaged the Mediterranean coasts from Gibraltar to the Bosphorus. The threat of a de-Christianised Europe was very real. In 1571, Pope Pius V formed the Holy League in conjunction with Spain, Venice and Genoa, in order to repulse the Ottoman incursion. Largely a sea borne alliance, it was led by Don Juan of Austria, who set out to meet the Ottoman fleet at the Gulf of Patras. Back at the Vatican, Pius V (surely influenced by the Dominicans, in which order he started his ecclesiastical life) urged the faithful to join him in praying the Rosary. After the decisive victory, the Pope ordered that the Rosary be recited at Mass in the Vatican every October 7th in celebration; his successor, Gregory XIII, formally established the Feast of the Most Holy Rosary in 1573 (the entire month of October is devoted to the Rosary today).

A very significant development took place in the fifteenth century when, in the Carthusian monasteries, the *clausulae* were developed – phrases added to the end of each of the 150 Aves.

Each *clausula* was a brief statement of faith drawn from the life of Christ, and was meditated upon in the Ave to which it was attached. This effectively transformed the Rosary from being a purely vocal prayer to becoming an aid to meditation.

Gradually, the *clausulae* were reduced to the fifteen mysteries of today, outlined in a book by the Dominican Luis de Granada, entitled *Rosario della sacratissima vergine Maria*, and printed in 1573.

Throughout the centuries, the Rosary continued in widespread use, as a prayer for the simple and the learned alike. In the 1940s and 1950s there was a tremendous surge of interest in the Rosary, pioneered by people like Bishop Fulton Sheen and Father Patrick Peyton, with his Family Rosary Crusade.

Vatican II, while enthusiastic in its recommendations about devotion to Mary, made no specific reference to the Rosary. Many people felt that the new emphasis on the liturgy was sweeping away all the old devotional practices, a perception reinforced by the Council's pronouncements: 'Popular devotions of the Christian people are warmly commended, provided they accord with the laws and norms of the church ... these devotions should be so drawn up that they harmonise with the liturgical seasons, accord with the sacred liturgy, are in some fashion derived from it and lead the people to it, since the liturgy by its very nature far surpasses any of them'.[2]

In 1969, efforts were made to harmonise the Rosary with the liturgy, and were not well received. The fact that some Marian feast days had been eliminated, and the importance of some others diminished, fuelled a perception that the Council was anti-Marian.

It may well have been in response to this perception that Paul VI wrote the apostolic letter *Marialis Cultus* (2 February 1974). This was a ringing endorsement of the Rosary as a powerful contemplative prayer drawing its motivating force from the liturgy and leading naturally back to it.[3] The letter also reinforced the contemplative nature of the Rosary.[4]

Introduction

'…thou hast created us for thyself, and our heart knows no rest, until it may repose in thee.' (St Augustine, *Confessions*, bk 1, ch 1)

This book has its origins in a dark place, where the light of my own faith was all but extinguished. My spiritual landscape was barren, unlit. I, the 'hollow man' stood aimlessly on its sterile surface. There comes a time in one's spiritual life where one can choose either to despair or to endure. Somehow, a phrase from Romans stayed in my memory: 'suffering produces endurance, and endurance produces character, and character produces hope, and hope does not disappoint us, because God's love has been poured into our hearts through the Holy Spirit which has been given to us'.[5]

By the light of the merest flicker of faith, I prayed. I don't know why I chose the Rosary. Even when my faith was strong, I didn't have a particular devotion to Our Lady. Perhaps the very tedium of the repetition suited my state of spiritual apathy. It was a half-hearted last-ditch effort: 'Here I am, Lord. What I'm saying doesn't mean much to me, but I leave it up to you to do something – if you're out there'.

I discovered how repetition, far from exteriorising prayer, could lead to interiorisation. It is hardly a new discovery. Long before the Rosary, there was the Litany of the Saints, one of the earliest forms of liturgical prayer. That the roots of the repetitive form of the Litany are even older is evident when one looks at Psalm 136, with its constant refrain 'for his steadfast love endures for ever'. This psalm was used in both public and private prayer. 'What else is the beating of the heart but repetition?' asks theologian Romano Guardini. ' What else is breathing but a repetition? Always the same in and out; but by breathing we live …

All life realises itself in the rhythm of external conditions and internal accomplishment'.[6]

Slowly – very slowly – the sheer repetition began to uncover layers of past belief. Images surfaced from the decades, images that touched me in the empty place where I was. Simeon, maintaining his faith in the coming of the Messiah despite centuries of silence – and then finding him in the most unlikely place. The extraordinary leap of faith made by the good thief. Joseph and Nicodemus emerging from the darkness to claim the body of him with whom they were terrified to be associated when living.

The echoes, weak at first and then increasingly strong, from the Old Testament: the nativity of Jesus – the 'star of Jacob' brought vividly to me the image of Jacob wrestling with God and refusing to let him go 'until you bless me'.[7] Like Jacob, I was striving with God. The annunciation, evoking Nazareth in its hilltop location overlooking the plain where Elijah confronted Ahab, brought up the buried memory of the still, small voice in which Elijah finally heard God.

And so it continued. The Rosary became a sort of living pilgrimage through the Old as well as the New Testament. The landscape constantly changed – sometimes one image, sometimes another would present itself. As I prayed, I continually saw endurance translate into hope.

The questions of accuracy raised by historical analysis were not obstacles. What mattered was the significance the ancient mind attached to its recording of events, not whether they happened as described. In any case, history is constantly revising itself. (It has, for instance, been commonly held in recent times that the nativity did not occur at Bethlehem; that there was no unusual star in the heavens at that time; that no census took place; and that the slaughter of the innocents was a myth. However, in the last ten years new research has been published describing a series of astral events culminating in a conjunction of Jupiter and Saturn which would have been clearly visible above Bethlehem in the year 7BC, and which would have been seen as of immense significance to Babylonian astrologers.[8] In February 2000, a mass grave of 100 infants was discovered at

Ashkelon, not far from Bethlehem. Early indications strongly suggest that the burial took place in the reign of Herod. The census referred to by Luke is generally believed to be the one carried out by Quirinius, which occurred at least a decade after Christ's birth.[9] However, history has shown that censuses took years to complete at that time, and one completed by Quirinius in AD 6-9 might well have commenced many years earlier.)

In the following chapters I have, therefore, not questioned historical accuracy. I have been guided instead by the significance that the scriptural writers attached to the events.

I have begun to realise that, within myself there is a space where the heart's desire is met.

Many of us live our entire lives without knowing this, and we seek our heart's desire in external things – relationships, work, distraction, addiction. 'And behold, thou wert within me, and I out of myself, where I made search for thee'.[10]

Sometimes, there is an aching feeling of loss, a desire to go home – without knowing where home is. Days can pass in numbness, broken occasionally by a fierce mental pain, or a piercing sense of sorrow, or a clutching anxiety in the pit of the stomach. My own reaction to that existential pain – and I am sure that my reaction is shared by many – has usually been to anaesthetise it as quickly as possible. But there comes a time when the anaesthetic wears off. Then we can either despair, or endure.

I have not been in that blessed space within myself where 'the Spirit himself intercedes for us with sighs too deep for words'.[11] However, I have at last – through the Rosary – reached an awareness that the space exists, and knowing that the place is there is at least a start in reaching it. Sometimes, like Columbus, we set out on a journey to a particular destination and find another place entirely. But if we never set out, how can we hope to arrive anywhere?

The further I travelled through the Rosary, the more I discovered. The past lived, and illuminated the present. David leaping before the Ark of the Covenant awakened in me the concept of

celebration; Ezekiel's eerie vision of the valley where the dry
bones were breathed upon, and clothed in flesh and life, opened
an avenue of hope; the image of the Ark of the Covenant moving
through the wilderness with the pillar of fire, awakened the belief that I, too, might at last find a way through my own wilderness. And, as I daily complete and recommence the journey of
the Rosary, through it all – increasingly lifting my own darkness
– reverberates the great declamation, old as Genesis, 'Let there
be light!'

The Joyful Mysteries

First Joyful Mystery: The Annunciation

Out of the Silence

For four hundred years, the so-called 'Silent Years', the voice of the prophets had been silent in Israel. Fifteen hundred years of communication from God to man through the scriptures seemed to have ended with the book of Malachi, the final book of the Old Testament. What a sombre note on which to end! The glorious kingdom for which the Jews have been waiting with such passionate expectation has not yet come. While the Babylonian captivity is over and the Temple has been rebuilt, the country is ravaged by famine and drought, and the people weighed down with unremitting hardship. Profoundly discouraged, Malachi's people have become distant from God, and he castigates them for their indifference.

However, Malachi's book does contain hope, and the promise of the Messiah – a Messiah who will be preceded by a messenger: 'Behold, I will send you Elijah the prophet.'

Four hundred years later, and within the space of six months, that long silence is shattered by two angelic visits, one to an elderly priest serving in the Temple at Jerusalem, the other to his wife's cousin, a girl of perhaps fourteen or fifteen years, living in an obscure village in Galilee.

Galilee would not have seemed a likely setting for the fulfilment of centuries of messianic prophecy. Years later the Pharisees, bent on the downfall of Jesus, will say: 'Search and you will see that no prophet is to rise from Galilee' (Jn 7:52). The village of Nazareth, completely insignificant in a country that was itself no bigger than Wales, is nowhere mentioned in the Old Testament. Low, flat-roofed houses built of bricks made from sun-baked mud and straw surrounded an open space, where the social intercourse of the village took place. Inside the houses, the floors would have been earthen, the light dim, and furnishings minimal.

Nazareth's hillside location overlooks the Plain of Jezreel where, eight hundred years earlier, King Ahab, husband of Jezebel – the archenemy of the prophet Elijah – coveted Naboth's vineyard. On this plain Elijah confronted Ahab, and upbraided him with the wickedness of his house, wringing repentance from the king and a relenting of God's anger against him (1 Kings 21). Mary would have been well familiar with the story of Elijah, whose towering presence dominates the Book of Kings. She, like all instructed Jews, would also have been keenly aware of the closing words of Malachi's book and its prophecy of the coming again of Elijah as forerunner to the Messiah. At the time Gabriel visits Mary, Mary's cousin Elizabeth is already carrying that forerunner, whom Jesus will describe in the words: '… he is Elijah who is to come' (Mt 11:14).

To this insignificant village, then, comes Gabriel, addressing the Galilean girl with the ringing salutation: 'Hail, O favoured one, the Lord is with you.' What a greeting to receive, and from what a messenger! This is Gabriel, who had recently visited Elizabeth's husband, Zechariah, and whose name – had he given it – would have been familiar to Mary as the angel who greeted the prophet Daniel with equally acclamatory words: 'O Daniel … you are greatly beloved' (Dan 9: 22-23). So the angel's visit links two people, born six hundred years apart: the prophet whose sweeping apocalyptic vision embraced the coming of the Messiah, and Mary of Nazareth, about to enter on her central role in the evolving redemptive process foretold by Daniel and his predecessors.

Of the dialogue in Luke's account of the annunciation, we tend only to remember the utter acceptance of God's will contained in Mary's words 'Behold the handmaid of the Lord; let it be to me according to your word.' It seems an inhumanly calm response to an unimaginable situation. But there is nothing calm about Mary's response to Gabriel's opening salutation. She was 'greatly troubled at the saying, and considered in her mind what sort of greeting this might be'.

It was hardly surprising that she should have been troubled. We are not told whether the angel actually appeared to her, or communicated in some other way. Either way, the sensation of the closeness of God's splendour must have been colossal.

The angel goes on to say: 'You will conceive in your womb and bear a son, and you shall call his name Jesus.' Jesus. Literally 'God is deliverance.' Any uncertainty about the purpose of the angel's visit must now be disappearing fast. The words that the angel goes on to speak are surely full of resonances for Mary. The whole body of Messianic prophecy lies behind them. So, when Gabriel speaks of the Lord God giving to this child 'the throne of his father David', and when he tells of one who will reign over the house of David forever, and of whose kingdom there will be no end, other voices must have been sounding almost simultaneously in Mary's ears: 'Of the increase of his government and of peace there will be no end, upon the throne of David, and over his kingdom, to establish it, and to uphold it with justice and with righteousness from this time forth and for evermore' (Is 9:7). Or: 'I will raise up for David a righteous branch, and he shall reign as king and deal wisely ... In his days Judah will be saved, and Israel will dwell securely' (Jer 23:5, 6). Or, again: '... the God of heaven will set up a kingdom which shall never be destroyed ... it shall stand forever' (Dan 2:44). Passages like these would have been familiar to any devout Jew, and it is not difficult to imagine the great crescendo of prophecy clamouring in Mary's subconscious, as the angel's words proclaim the fulfilment of the ancient promises. By now, for Mary, there can be no doubt that the son of whom the angel speaks is to be the Messiah.

She has little time to assimilate these tidings before something yet more remarkable follows. In all the Messianic prophecies, there is nothing to suggest that the Promised One would be born in any way other than according to the laws of nature, and there is very little to suggest his divinity. While the expression 'Son of Man' frequently occurs in the Old Testament and, indeed, will often be used by Jesus when speaking of himself, there is nothing to prepare Mary for a literal interpretation of the words Gabriel will shortly use, 'Son of God'.

Mary asks how she will conceive 'since I have no husband'. It is a curious question, given that we have already been told she is betrothed. In some translations, however, the words used by Gabriel are 'behold, you are about to conceive' – and perhaps the explanation for Mary's question lies here. If the angel is suggesting the conception is to be immediate and if, for example, Joseph was away for Nazareth for a time, then Mary's question becomes more understandable.

The angel's reply tells her that this child is to be conceived as no child ever had been before: 'The Holy Spirit will come upon you, and the power of the Most High will overshadow you; therefore the child to be born will be called holy, the Son of God.' And then Mary says: 'Behold, I am the handmaid of the Lord; let it be to me according to your word'. As she embarks on her mission of bringing into the world the Light of the World, her words echo God's own words in the opening chapter of Genesis when, on the first day of creation, he floods the heavens and the earth with his radiance as he utters the mighty words: 'Let there be light'.

Prayer

Lord, when the silence seems heavy and impenetrable, I recall how it can be broken at the most unexpected time and in the most unexpected circumstances. I must be still enough to hear your voice; courageous enough to act on it.

Mary of Nazareth, I struggle in darkness. I, too, was born and came into the world for a purpose. That purpose will not be revealed to me as dramatically and unambiguously as it was to you. No angelic messenger will address me as I go about my daily business. The word of God will come to me in no clarion call. Perhaps you heard it so clearly because of your sinlessness. There was no unnecessary clamour drowning out his message.

If I am to hear the word of God it would perhaps be more realistic for me to look to a different precedent than your experience. And where better to look than to the story of Elijah, whose presence resonates throughout the great story of redemption?

After his forty days in the wilderness, Elijah finally hears the voice of God on the holy mountain of Horeb – not in the mighty wind that rent the mountains, nor in the earthquake, not in the consuming fire. It is a 'still small voice' (1 Kings 19:12) that Elijah hears in the entrance to his cave. In the noise and distraction of my roller-coaster life, I need to create a quietness where I can listen, a space where I will not be 'distracted with much serving', and 'anxious and troubled about many things' but will be alive to the fact – as another Mary was – that 'one thing is needful' (Lk 10:41, 42).

Grant that this great prayer of the Rosary may be my pathway to God's holy mountain. Help me to set aside, even for this brief period each day, the glory and the tragedy of this world. Let each contemplated mystery bring me a step further into the wilderness where all the familiar solaces and distractions are missing. Help me climb, with resolution and endurance, God's holy mountain and, above all, let me be still when I arrive. Help me to listen in stillness and accept in faith.

Second Joyful Mystery: The Visitation

'Yes!'

Before the angel leaves Mary, he tells her: 'And behold, your kinswoman Elizabeth in her old age has also conceived a son; and this is the sixth month with her who was called barren. For with God, nothing will be impossible' (Lk 1:36, 37).

Once again, we are hurled back to the beginning of the Old Testament, where another elderly woman, Sarah, conceives in her old age. And when Sarah laughs disbelievingly, asking: 'Shall I indeed bear a child, now that I am old?' the Lord in return asks Abraham: 'Is anything too hard for the Lord?' (Gen 18:13, 14). The story of Sarah must surely have leaped to Mary's mind as soon as she heard the angel's words. We think not only of Sarah, but of Sarah's son Isaac. This only son came close to being sacrificed by his father Abraham, but symbolically returned from death. (St Paul says that God, 'figuratively speaking, did receive (Isaac) back' from the dead. Heb 11:19.) Isaac thus prefigures the death and resurrection – although Mary does not know this yet – of another Only Son.

It is little wonder that Mary 'arose and went with haste into the hill country' to see Elizabeth! With Elizabeth, after all, lay potential corroboration of Mary's own astounding news and, more especially, somebody with whom to discuss it. Somebody who had herself experienced a virtually unprecedented unbending of the laws of nature.

Picture the journey to Elizabeth's house. It would have taken about four days, and Mary would have travelled in some form of convoy for safety. However many people were in the caravan, Mary must have been isolated in her own thoughts, isolated as no human being had ever been before. Did she doubt her own recollection of events? Did she wonder if she could have imagined the whole? With whom could she possibly share her story?

Her heart must have been pounding as she paused on Elizabeth's threshold. As she calls out a gentle, tentative greeting to her cousin, back comes the extraordinary response: 'Blessed are you among women, and blessed is the fruit of your womb! And why is this granted to me, that the mother of my Lord should come to me?' (Lk 1:42, 43)

Mary's mind must be in tumult. Here is her cousin evidently aware of Mary's situation, so shortly after the angel's visit. If further validation of the angel's message is needed, it is not long in coming. Elizabeth's next words suggest that she was out of Mary's visual range when Mary first entered the house: '... when the voice of your greeting came to my ears ...' We can imagine Mary, her mind seething with questions regarding Elizabeth's greeting, watch Elizabeth come into view. Moving slowly and heavily, the unmistakable fact of her advanced pregnancy is revealed to Mary's gaze as she concludes her sentence: '... when the voice of your greeting came to my ears, the babe in my womb leaped for joy.' Probably thinking of her sceptical husband, or possibly of Sarah and Abraham, we can hear her add in a repentant undertone: 'And blessed is she who believed that there would be a fulfilment of what was spoken to her from the Lord' (Lk 1:44, 45).

Elizabeth knows that her son is destined for greatness. He is to go before the Lord 'in the spirit and power of Elijah, to turn the hearts of fathers to their children ... to make ready for the Lord a people prepared' (Lk 1:17). She cannot have failed to relate these words to the closing words of the Book of Malachi – the last words God was to utter to his people through the prophets of the Old Testament: 'Behold, I will send you Elijah the prophet before the great and terrible day of the Lord comes. And he will turn the hearts of fathers to their children and the hearts of children to their fathers' (Mal 4:5, 6). Once again, Gabriel's visit and Gabriel's words span the four hundred 'Silent Years'. The air is alive with prophecy entering fulfilment.

And what a dramatic moment for Mary as her elderly cousin emerges from the shadows of the house! If there had been the faintest doubt in Mary's mind – and she would not have been human had there not been – it has now vanished. Her own destiny is confirmed by the visible fact of Elizabeth's post-menopausal pregnancy. Here is where Mary's true greatness begins to appear. Her spontaneous reaction to this sealing of the angel's message and her own awe-inspiring destiny is exultant. Not a trace of fear, of ambivalence, of hesitation marks her response.

The *Magnificat* is a ringing, confident, jubilant 'Yes!' from Mary to God.

There are many resonances in the *Magnificat* of the joyful song of Hannah (1 Sam 2:1-10), yet another Old Testament woman who had to wait long for a child. It is a fitting evocation: the child whose birth Hannah was celebrating was Samuel, last of the judges. Samuel would anoint David and establish his kingship. Mary's son will inherit that kingship, transforming it into an everlasting reign.

Mary has no difficulty in reconciling humility with greatness. The Lord 'has regarded the low estate of his handmaiden. For behold, henceforth all generations will call me blessed'. It is an amazing claim, by any standards. From a young girl, a carpenter's fiancée living in a Galilean backwater, it is staggering. But it is fulfilled, daily, two thousand years on in countless daily reiterations of 'Hail Mary'.

There is no false humility in Mary's prayer. There is the true humility of knowing that all that is being accomplished in her is being accomplished by God, 'for he who is mighty has done great things for me' (Lk 1:49). Mary makes no effort to minimise this greatness. She accepts it – fully, joyfully and expectantly. If the events of the annunciation demonstrated Mary's faith, then the visitation, with its great song of praise, is a glorious expression of Mary's hope.

It is a visionary prayer. Mary sees the fulfilment of the prophecies: God's everlasting victory over evil, his succour for the poor, his never-ending assistance to Israel 'in remembrance of his mercy, as he spoke to our fathers, to Abraham and to his posterity for ever'.

Let us look at the scene once more, for it is profoundly moving. There they stand, the two cousins – undoubtedly in close embrace – tears of joy running down their faces. Each conscious of her remarkable destiny. Each filled with expectation. And the scene is peopled with a great gathering of shadowy figures – Abraham and Sarah, laughingly disbelieving of the good news God brought to them; Isaac, the only son who would be offered as a sacrifice, and the person with whom God establishes his first covenant with his people; Hannah jubilant at the birth of Samuel, the prophet who will anoint the great King David – whose kingship Jesus will inherit and transmute into an everlasting reign; and dark Malachi who, from the depth of his desolation, can still hold out the promise of the new Elijah.

Prophecy is becoming revelation. This is a meeting, after all, not of two people, but of four. The Forerunner and the Promised One are physically present, each in the womb of his mother. Of that other only son, God said to Abraham: '… Sarah your wife shall bear you a son, and you shall call his name Isaac. I will establish my covenant with him as an everlasting covenant for his descendants after him' (Gen 17:19). Of Isaac's father, Abraham, Jesus himself will say: 'Truly, truly I say to you, before Abraham was, I am' (Jn 8:58). Here, at a fixed point in time and place, a young Galilean girl carries within her womb One 'who is and who was and who is to come, the Almighty' (Rev 1:8).

We pause now, on the threshold of Elizabeth's house, at a remarkable moment in time: the New Testament covenant of God with his people is about to begin.

Prayer

'And blessed is she who believed that there would be a fulfilment of what was spoken to her from the Lord'.

You speak to me from the whole of scripture, Lord, and yet I remain deaf to your words, refusing (from apathy? from false modesty? from fear?) to believe in the fulfilment that awaits me in discovering your will for me and doing it.

Why is it, Lord, that I seem so unable to combine faith with hope? Why is it that my faith can so often be a joyless thing, a belief that the only way to you is along a *via dolorosa*? Why is it that whenever we hear the words 'God's will be done', it is almost invariably on some sorrowful or tragic occasion? Do we ever hear them at times of celebration? Christ, urging the people to keep God's commandments, adds: 'These things I have spoken to you, that my joy may be in you, and that your joy may be full' (Jn 15:11).

Mary had no such problem. So I ask you, Lord, to give me Mary's confidence and generosity of spirit. I ask not just to listen to your voice and do your will, but to do it joyfully and fearlessly. I want to answer your call with an exultant 'Yes!', secure in the knowledge that as I move into the unknown my journey will be made radiant by your transfiguring presence, and that 'thy hand shall lead me, and thy right hand shall hold me' (Ps 139:10).

Third Joyful Mystery: The Nativity

'… and there was light'

'In those days a decree went out from Caesar Augustus that all the world should be enrolled … And all went to be enrolled, each to his own city'(Lk 2:1-3). Joseph, 'being of the house of David', sets off for David's city, Bethlehem, accompanied by Mary.

The Emperor Augustus' intervention in the lives of Mary and Joseph would have clarified something that must have been puzzling them greatly. Throughout Mary's pregnancy, we can be certain that Mary and Joseph would have been studying the scriptures as never before. Nowhere, in the whole of scripture, does humble Nazareth receive so much as a mention. It must have seemed a most unlikely birthplace for the Messiah.

But once the Emperor had set them on the royal road to Bethlehem, Micah's prophecy would have rung in the ears of Mary and Joseph: 'But you, O Bethlehem Ephrathah, who are little to be among the clans of Judah, from you shall come forth for me one who is to be ruler in Israel, whose origin is from of old, from ancient days' (Mic 5:2). This prophecy about the birthplace of a Messiah is one which the chief priests will remember and will share with Herod when he asks them where the Christ is to be born (Mt 2:5). The part of the prophecy which indicates that the Messiah will pre-exist his own birth is one that we remember when Jesus tells the Jews: 'before Abraham was, I am' (Jn 8:58).

The earliest mention of Bethlehem in the Bible occurs in Genesis: Rachel, hard-won and beloved wife of Jacob, dies in childbirth at Ephrathah (Gen 35:16-19). But, for Mary, a more vivid scriptural association will be a later one: to Bethlehem came the Gentile, Ruth. Here she met and married her Jewish husband, Boaz and bore a son, Obed, father of Jesse, father of David. Generations later, Mary's own son, the new and greater David, will break down many more barriers between Jew and Gentile.

At Bethlehem, the prophet Samuel summoned Jesse and his

sons to choose the Lord's anointed from among them and make him king. One after another of Jesse's seven fine sons passed before Samuel with no intimation that the Lord has chosen. Finally, Jesse admits to an eighth son: 'There remains yet the youngest, but behold, he is keeping the sheep.' David is then brought to Samuel, and the Lord immediately says of the shepherd boy: 'Arise, anoint him; for this is he' (1 Sam 16:1-12).

Now, thirty generations from the time of King David, another Shepherd King is going to be born in Bethlehem. His mother, very close to her time, sets out on the 70-mile journey. For any expectant mother facing the birth of her first child, this is a time of heartstopping anticipation, of devouring curiosity about the child who is about to be born. What new mother has not been seized time and again with excitement at the prospect of meeting, finally, this tiny being whom her body has harboured for nine long months?

Mary of Nazareth knew more about the baby she was carrying than do other mothers. She had the whole of scripture to enlighten her: 'There shall come forth a root from the stump of Jesse, and a branch shall grow out of his roots. And the spirit of the Lord shall rest upon him, the spirit of wisdom and understanding, the spirit of counsel and might ... him shall the nations seek, and his dwellings shall be glorious' (Is 11:1-2, 10).

There was nothing glorious about the birthplace in David's city of the 'Lion of the Tribe of Judah, the Root of David' (Rev 5:5). Bethlehem was thronged for the census. The inn, with people sleeping several to a room, can have offered no possibility of the privacy Mary urgently needed. By now, she was in labour; it is not difficult to imagine some kindly woman bringing her to the one place she could be delivered of her baby in peace. And since that place was not already occupied in a town where space was clearly at a premium, it is not hard to imagine just how basic a shelter it must have been.

This was surely not the snug little stable of our Christmas cribs, packed with clean, warm straw. It was more likely to have been a cave, barely sheltered from the elements, with a clay floor well trodden by animals. In the most comfortless imaginable surroundings, assisted by strangers, Mary of Nazareth is delivered of the child who was to be called Wonderful Counsellor, Almighty God, Everlasting Father, Prince of Peace. Amid the dim light provided by torches flickering in the many draughts, she gives birth to the Light of the World, the Only Son, loved by God 'before the foundation of the world' (Jn 17:24). On this most holy night, the Word becomes flesh, and dwells among us.

Outside, shepherds are keeping watch. Suddenly, the sky above them explodes into blazing light as 'an angel of the Lord appeared to them, and the glory of the Lord shone around them' (Lk 2:9). With the song of celestial multitudes ringing in their ears 'Glory be to God in the highest', the dazed shepherds make their way to the place where the baby lies. These are his first visitors.

Mary must have wondered greatly. There was little in scripture to prepare her for the fact that the Messiah's kingdom was not to be of this world. She can surely not have anticipated that this child, fulfilment of centuries of expectation, would be born in squalor. And his first visitors! Shepherds were among the lowest of the low in Jewish society – known for their violence, dishonesty, disrespect for the law. They lived lives of utter deprivation. We can imagine them, wild unkempt men, wrapped in their filthy rags, gathering somewhat timidly at the entrance to the cave.

Shepherds visiting a shepherd. A thousand years earlier, the Lord said to David: 'You shall be shepherd of my people Israel' (2 Sam 5:2). Now, in the most meagre shelter in David's city, lies he who '… will feed his flock like a shepherd, he will gather the lambs in his arms, he will carry them in his bosom, and gently lead those that are with young' (Is 40:11). Had Isaiah lived to see this day, the sight of the infant in his mother's arms must surely have recalled the closing chapter of his towering book: here he foretold the comfort and calm of the messianic age: 'As one whom his mother comforts, so I will comfort you' (Is 66:13).

Even as the shepherds gather in worship, more visitors are well on their way. These, to the Jewish establishment, would have been just as unorthodox in their own way as the shepherds – being Gentiles. The three wise men, the *magoi*, come from Persia? Media? Babylon? They have seen Christ's star in the east, and follow it unerringly to his birthplace.

Shepherds came to see a shepherd; the wise men followed a star to see 'the root and offspring of David, the bright morning star' (Rev 22:16). The 'bright morning star' described in the closing chapter of the Bible was foretold a millennium and a half before, in the Book of Numbers. This book is called in Hebrew

'In the Wilderness', as it traces the forty years' wanderings of the Israelites from Mount Sinai to the plains of Moab. In the midst of the desolation of these dark years, the light of prophecy still shines: the gentile prophet Balaam, filled with the Spirit of God, predicts: 'A star shall come out of Jacob, and a sceptre shall rise out of Israel' (Num 24:17). The sceptre represents the reign of David; the star of Jacob is the greater David, who is Jesus. 'I see him, but not now,' says Balaam; 'I behold him, but not nigh.'

But now he is nigh. He is born in the night, with his own star blazing above him, and the skies above the shepherds are incandescent with light. Within the dimness of the stable lies the Lord who, as a pillar of cloud by day and a pillar of fire by night, led the Israelites from Egyptian slavery to freedom. Incarnate, he has come again to bring his people from darkness into light. As we gaze into the manger, at the tiny creature who is given to us 'as a light to the nations' (Is 42:6), we can only whisper 'come, let us adore him'.

Prayer

'...the light has come into the world, and men loved darkness rather than light...' I have known my moments of exultation. Like the shepherds, my night watches have at times been radiantly illuminated. But alas! How quickly I found myself back at the wayside, immersed in fear and ravaged by anxiety. The flashes of exultation faded fast, plunging me into a darkness even more dense and black than that which went before. I am indeed the lost sheep, without even the faith to cry out for her shepherd.

Help me to realise that the light is there for me to find, if I want to find it. Help me to understand, as David in his dying words urged Solomon, that if I seek the Lord he will be found by me. Help me have the perseverance and confidence of the Magi, who were willing to travel far into the unknown in pursuit of light and, when they found it in the most unprepossessing surroundings, did not let any preconceptions cause them to falter. Help me to have the tenacity of Jacob who, as he wrestled with God, cried out: 'I will not let you go, unless you bless me'.

It was not in the blazing night skies that the shepherds found the Light of the World, but in the dimness and barrenness of a cave. Somewhere within me, I must find a quiet, uncluttered place wherein I may seek him. Luke tells us that you, Mary, 'kept all these things, pondering them in her heart'. It is an important message. I can learn about God with my brain, but I can only *know* him in my heart. Too often, I fear the emptiness, the darkness, the silence within me. Yet, it is there that the Spirit lives and moves, working even when my prayers seem most arid. Help me to go daily into the quiet of my own heart, and help me to meet God there, in love and adoration.

Fourth Joyful Mystery: The Presentation in the Temple

The Shadow of the Cross

Forty days have passed since the birth of Jesus. These have been days of ritual purification for Mary, at the end of which time she is obliged to offer sacrifice. She and Joseph also have to present their first-born son to the Lord.

This presentation of the first-born son was a legacy of the great Passover, when God's people were freed from their 280 years of bondage in Egypt. As they sprinkled their door lintels with the blood of a lamb without blemish, the Israelites were spared by the avenging angel who slew all the first born in the Land of Egypt. 'And when the Lord brings you into the land of the Canaanites', Moses told his people on the day of their liberation, '... you shall set apart to the Lord all that first opens the womb. All the firstlings of your cattle that are males shall be the Lord's ... Every first born of man among your sons you will redeem' (Ex 13:12-13).

Now, over a thousand years later, Mary and Joseph set off to the Temple to observe the law. The redemption of the first-born took the form of a money offering: the child literally had to be bought back from God. But this is one first-born child whose life will not be purchased, despite the offering that Joseph will make. This life is God's from the start, and the long shadow of the cross reaches even to these first weeks. Among the crowds who surge daily through the Temple, how many on this day notice the little Nazarene family on their extraordinary mission of presenting the Son to his own Father, redeeming the Redeemer, and purifying her who is already immaculate! Most will not give the young country carpenter and his wife a second glance. Yet Mary is cradling in her arms the Lamb of God, whose own blood will deliver his people.

'Now there was a man in Jerusalem, whose name was Simeon, and this man was righteous and devout, looking for the consolation of Israel, and the Holy Spirit was upon him,' writes

Luke (Lk 2:25). Simeon was one of those for whom the long silence of the prophets had done nothing to reduce his eager expectation of the Messiah. He was a man of intense spirituality, so close to God that it had been revealed to him that he would not die before he had seen the Messiah. Now, as Mary and Joseph set out for the Temple, Simeon, too, sets out – his steps driven by the Holy Spirit.

It must be a moment of great drama when Simeon forges his way through the milling crowds and goes directly to Mary, taking the baby Jesus in his arms. The Second and Third Persons of the Holy Trinity are present in an extraordinarily immediate way as Simeon, utterly filled with the Holy Spirit, bursts into prophetic speech.

The opening words are almost one long exhalation of relief, of expectation realised, hope fulfilled: 'Lord, now lettest thou thy servant depart in peace, according to thy word; for mine eyes have seen thy salvation which thou hast prepared in the presence of all peoples, a light for revelation to the Gentiles, and for glory to thy people Israel' (Lk 2:29-32).

Why did his father and mother 'marvel' at what Simeon said? It can hardly be that they are not prepared, by now, for the knowledge that this child is a child apart. It can hardly be that they are surprised that a total stranger should know this – after all, have they not had the experience of the shepherds to tell them that the good news is being – however strangely and selectively – communicated? It must surely be at the reference to the Gentiles. The reference would be bewildering in itself to orthodox Jews, but must have been doubly so since it actually precedes reference to the Jews!

To the Jews, the Messiah was uniquely theirs. He would deliver Israel and establish a kingdom that would not be destroyed. Gentiles would have formed no obvious part of this kingdom: there is little in the Old Testament to prepare anyone for the fact that the kingdom of Christ will so wholeheartedly embrace Gentiles. Little, but not nothing: Isaiah does, on at least two occasions, talk about the Messiah as 'a light to the gentiles' (Is 42:6; 49:6).

Simeon blesses Mary and Joseph then, but not Jesus. He knows that Jesus can have no need of his blessing. He goes on to speak exclusively to Mary – does he, then, realise that Joseph is not the father in this family? 'Behold, this child is set for the fall and rising of many in Israel, and for a sign that is spoken against (and a sword will pierce your own soul also), that thoughts out of many hearts may be revealed' (Luke 2:34, 35).

Here it is, then, the stark choice which belief in Christ presents: he, who is the keystone for some, will be a stumbling stone for others, 'both a sanctuary and a stone of offence, and a rock of stumbling' (Is 8:14). In Christ's own words: 'The very stone which the builders rejected has become the head of the corner ... and he who falls on this stone will be broken to pieces' (Mt 21:42, 44). Once having known him, there is no halfway house: 'He who is not with me is against me, and he who does not gather with me scatters' (Mt 12:30). We can embrace him or resist him; we cannot say 'yes' and 'no' at once for, as St Paul says, 'in him it is always Yes. For all the promises of God find their Yes in him' (2 Cor 1:19, 20).

But the closer we come, the greater the potential fall. The human psyche is ingenious at finding ways to rationalise retreat and betrayal. Love which turns to hatred is possibly the most dangerous and fanatical of all emotions. Jesus himself will be betrayed with a kiss of friendship. The pain of that betrayal and its horrible consequences will drive a sword deep into Mary's heart.

There is another sword in this story. 'Thoughts out of many hearts ' will be revealed. Even those thoughts that we had hidden from ourselves. Total truth is demanded; there is no room for compromise. 'For the word of God is living and active, sharper than any two-edged sword, piercing to the division of soul and spirit, of joints and marrow, and discerning the thoughts and intentions of the heart. And before him no creature is hidden, but all are open and laid bare to the eyes of him with whom we have to do' (Heb 4:12, 13).

Here in the Temple is the Word of God, incarnate. Simeon, in his prophecy, speaks of a sword. The baby cannot speak yet, but much later he, too, will speak of a sword: 'I have not come to bring peace, but a sword' (Mt 10:34). This sword is the sword that will divide his followers from anything which impedes their progress towards him.

Here, within weeks of his birth, we are confronted with the joy and the pain which following him entails. We are made aware of the challenge that faces us: the clarity of vision that is demanded of us, and the courage and commitment without which we cannot realise that vision. We must see clearly: 'If your eye is sound,' Jesus says in the Sermon on the Mount, 'your whole body will be full of light; but if your eye is not sound, your whole body will be full of darkness. If then the light in you is darkness, how great is the darkness! No one can serve two masters' (Mt 6:22-24).

As Anna, also filled with the Holy Spirit, joins the small group with exultant thanksgiving, Mary has much to ponder. The cold blade of fear must surely have touched her heart with Simeon's words. Troubling words, with flashes of joy – light and glory, contradiction and division, thanksgiving and sorrow. Her mind may be in turmoil, but she does not allow herself to be distracted from performing everything that the law of the Lord requires, before returning to Nazareth. 'And the child grew and became strong, filled with wisdom, and the favour of God was upon him' (Lk 2:40).

Prayer

Lord, in Simeon – as with the Magi – I see hope triumphant, hope richly rewarded. The years of waiting – the centuries before he himself was born and the long years that he had lived – did not blunt the edge of his faith. His hope and yearning left him alive to the prompting of God, ready to hear it when it came. Grant that I may learn from him.

When that two-edged sword cleaves my heart, grant that the thoughts revealed will be good and true. Grant that it may always be 'Yes' with me, and never 'yes and no'.

Give me the courage to commit.

Perhaps, Mary, I might learn a very useful lesson from the care with which you observed the rituals surrounding the presentation and purification, after your meeting with Simeon and Anna. Despite the extraordinary and disturbing utterances that you have just heard, you go on to do 'everything according to the law of the Lord'. Perhaps through the very formality of these observances, the tumult in your mind was calmed and your clarity restored.

In praying the Rosary, I am seeking something similar. The repetition of the words is a form of release, a gateway that allows me to enter and explore the mysteries, dwelling on different elements at different times. Some days, I feel as though I am observing a piece of film; but at other times, I am there in the middle of the event, seeing, and above all listening. But there are too many times when I do not want to listen, for fear of what I might hear. I can hardly read the Lord's words as written by Jeremiah without an overwhelming sense of guilt: ' I have spoken to them and they have not listened, I have called to them and they have not answered' (Jer 35:17).

Simeon listened to the prompting of the Spirit, which led him to the Temple on that day. Perhaps I am afraid that I will be led somewhere I do not want to go. Help me, Mary, to have less fear and greater trust. You didn't allow the dreadful threat of future sword-like sorrow to stop you doing the things that had to be done, nor to hinder you in going back to Nazareth and bringing up your child – and what joy there must have been in that! Let me be at all times generously alive to the direction of the Spirit so that at the end of my days I, like Simeon, can utter a *'nunc dimittis'* from my heart.

Fifth Joyful Mystery:
The Finding in the Temple

The Three Days' Loss

A Passover. Followed by three days' loss, it presages that sombre, magnificent Passover twenty-one years later.

Each year, Mary and Joseph made the 70-mile journey to Jerusalem to celebrate the feast of the Passover. When he was twelve years old Jesus went up with them – although he was still not of an age when he would be bound to observe the laws of the Torah. Nor was Mary obliged to go, but it was not unusual for women, with their younger children, to accompany their husbands.

The road they take is the same road they had taken twelve years earlier for Bethlehem, which lies five miles south of Jerusalem. They would have travelled in a large party, making the journey over a period of four days, and chanting the processional psalms as they went. We can imagine the boy Jesus as he first sees the walls of the Temple. This is one of the wonders of the ancient world – a vast building, the whole enclosure 144,000 square metres in size; columns and porticoes soaring to heights unimagined at the time, covered in gold and silver so dazzling in the sunlight that it hurt the eye.

But greater than the external splendour are the powerful evocations of Israel's past: the temple that David longed to build, but which was instead constructed by his son, Solomon, to house the Ark of the Covenant – to replace the tent which had contained it though the weary years of the Exodus. The temple was destroyed by Nebuchaddnezzar at the commencement of the Babylonian captivity; rebuilt by Judas Maccabaeus and destroyed again, this time by the Romans; and finally rebuilt by Herod. Magnificent though the temple is, its very heart – the Holy of Holies – stands empty. The Ark of the Covenant is missing since the time of the first destruction. The temple itself, still being worked on in the lifetime of Jesus, will be destroyed utterly four years after its completion.

Now he gazes at it – he who is himself the Holy of Holies. He who will be the everlasting temple. He must feel a shiver of joy as he hears the opening lines of Psalm 122, which all pilgrims sang as soon as the temple came into sight: 'I was glad when they said to me, "Let us go to the house of the Lord!"'

On the first day of the feast the paschal lamb is sacrificed by the head of the family or, if the family is not large enough (no fewer than ten and no more than twenty could eat the paschal meal together), the head of the group. Jesus would surely have accompanied Joseph to the temple to see their lamb purchased and ritually slain. Together, the family celebrate the institution of God's covenant with his people established 1,300 years earlier. How much does Jesus know of the Passover which will follow in his 33rd year, when he himself will be the sacrifice, slain and offered up, and in whose redeeming blood a new covenant will be established between God and man? Is he just like any small boy, filled with the excitement and the novelty of entering a man's world, or does the shadow of death lie across his path?

Then there is the great drama of the feast itself – all flame and shadow in its recollection of the plague of fire and hail, the three days' blackness, the nocturnal ceremonial meal eaten in haste as the avenging angel passed over the houses marked with the blood of a lamb.

When the feast is over, Mary and Joseph set off on the return journey to Nazareth, unaware that Jesus has remained behind in Jerusalem. That terrible awareness comes when, at the end of the long day's travelling, the men and women reunite. Each had thought him to be with the other.

At first, Mary and Joseph must have supposed that he was elsewhere in the travelling party. But then comes the dawning realisation that he is not there, and that he has not been seen all day. We can imagine their frantic questioning of everyone in the group. And then, the awful wait. It is nightfall; there can be no question of setting off to Jerusalem until daylight. What a night Mary and Joseph must have spent, racked with dread! And what a journey the next day, stopping at every point of the road to ask if he had been seen!

Then, back in Jerusalem, there follow two more days of gnawing fear. This is, after all, a teeming city full of danger for an unprotected child. Children are easily sold into slavery. The parents' blood must run cold at the possibilities.

One can see them, endlessly retracing their steps, checking at every place they had been during their Passover stay. And then they come to the temple. Mary may be remembering that other occasion when she brought Jesus there, as a tiny baby. Now, weighed down with grief, she must be thinking of Simeon's grim prophecy. The chances of finding the little boy after three days' fruitless searching must now seem slim. The sword of sorrow is twisting deeper and deeper into her heart.

Then, the discovery! Perhaps Mary and Joseph at first glance only cursorily at the group of elders concentrated around someone who is questioning them. Perhaps something – an intonation in the clear young voice, or a glimpse of a deeply familiar profile – rivets them to the spot. Then, wave upon wave of relief, tumultuous joy, mingled with the universal reaction of any parent to a child who has gone missing: 'Son, why have you treated us so?'

We can imagine how Mary whispers the words of reproach, her cheek, wet with tears, pressed against that of her son. 'Behold, your father and I have been looking for you anxiously.' Jesus, in his first recorded words, responds: 'How is it that you sought me? Did you not know that I must be in my Father's house?' (Lk 2:49).

'Must be'. There is a greater obedience demanded of this boy than that due to his earthly parents. Already, he has a sense of his divine mission. The word 'must' will recur in his utterances, in the context of his huge task of redemption: 'The Son of Man must suffer many things' (Lk 9:22); 'I must preach the good news of the kingdom of God' (Lk 4:43); 'I have other sheep, that are not of this fold; I must bring them also ...' (Jn 10:16); '... so must the Son of man be lifted up' (Jn 3:14).

There is no apology for the harrowing concern he has caused them. Yet this is a child on whom the favour of God manifestly rested and who can, until now, have caused his parents no anxiety. There is a calm assumption that the work he had to do in his Father's house superseded the normal obedience of a child to its parents. The same insistence on the precedence of God's work will be found many years later, when the adult Jesus stresses: 'He who loves father or mother more than me is not worthy of me' (Mt 10:37).

'And they did not understand the saying which he spoke to them' (Lk 2:50). Is it that Mary does not understand yet just how literally Gabriel's words were meant when he told her, at the annunciation, that her child would be called the 'Son of God'? One thing must have been clear: the house to which Jesus was referring was certainly not Joseph's house. The Father to whom he referred was not Joseph. Or are they surprised at his surprise? He takes it for granted that they should have known where to find him.

It is a completely isolated episode in the childhood of Jesus. Immediately after, he places himself in unreserved subjection to Joseph and Mary: 'And he went down with them and came to Nazareth, and was obedient to them ... and Jesus increased in wisdom and in stature, and in favour with God and man' (Lk 2:51-52).

We have had a glimpse into his future. There will be nothing else recorded for another eighteen years. In the next and, indeed, the last recorded interchange between Mary and Jesus, his obedience to her will bring him across the threshold separating the 'hidden years' from his public life. At the wedding feast of Cana, she will tell her son: 'They have no wine'. He will reply: 'My hour has not yet come' (Jn 2:3-4). But he immediately goes on to work the miracle that she clearly seeks of him.

His entrance into the public arena brings him back to the temple. This visit is very far removed from the visit of the exceptional boy who aroused such admiration in his hearers. Now, he makes his mark in a very different way, entering the temple as an avenging and a cleansing force, overturning the tables of the money changers, driving out sheep and oxen. Given the crowds who would be plying their lucrative trade there, we would expect them to have made short shrift of one disruptive presence, a seeming madman from the provinces. What made them flee before him? We can only imagine that that glimpse of divine mission, which flashes through the episode of the finding in the temple, is revealed more nakedly here. His own disciples are forcibly reminded of the words of one of the great messianic psalms: 'zeal for thy house has consumed me' (Ps 69:9). This is Jesus again in his Father's house and declaring, with blazing fury, 'you shall not make my Father's house a house of trade' (Jn 2:16).

Prayer

Perhaps, in all my seeking of Jesus, I do not stop to reflect that I may sometimes best find him in his Father's house. This is the house to which the Holy Spirit led Simeon with unerring steps and where Simeon found his heart's desire. This is where Mary and Joseph found blessed relief after the torment of loss. In its quietness maybe I can be still and enter that other temple wherein the Holy Spirit dwells and which is, unbelievably, within myself.

If I can begin to assimilate this amazing reality, perhaps I can open myself to even greater wonder: 'If a man loves me, he will keep my word, and my Father will love him and we will come to him and make our home with him' (Jn 14:23). Strange to think that after all the restless seeking, all the draining journeys, all the spent effort, the end of the journey is where I began it – within myself. Perhaps I will have to take that temple by storm like the adult Jesus, or by gentle questioning like the child. But I will certainly never take it without trust.

Mary, you made a distraught entrance to the temple in Jerusalem, seeking him whom you had lost. Help me to realise that if I go to the temple of the Holy Spirit within me, I go – unlike you – with the certainty of finding Jesus there.

The Sorrowful Mysteries

First Sorrowful Mystery:
The Agony in the Garden

From Eden to Gethsemane

Man's first fall from grace took place in a garden. Now, the great act of redemption begins in another garden. It has been a long journey from Eden to Gethsemane.

'And when they had sung a hymn, they went out to the Mount of Olives' (Mk 14:26). The antiphonal singing of Psalms 113-118 at the conclusion of the Passover liturgy must have pierced Jesus with their immediacy: 'The snares of death encompassed me; the pangs of Sheol laid hold on me; I suffered distress and anguish' (Ps 116:3).

He has celebrated his last Passover. In that meal, he has given to his disciples the cup of the new covenant between God and man. He now sets out to ratify that covenant with his own blood.

Before entering his public life, Jesus was led into the wilderness by the Holy Spirit and there encountered and overcame temptation. Before choosing the Twelve, 'he went out to the mountain to pray; and all night he continued in prayer to God' (Lk 6:12). In prayer on a mountain he was transfigured and his majesty revealed to Peter, James and John: '... we were eyewitnesses of his majesty' (2 Peter 1:16). At various stages throughout his public life, he felt this need to go alone into the hills and pray. Again and again, he drew his strength from prayer.

Now, once more, he goes into a quiet mountain place and tells his apostles: 'Sit here, while I pray' (Mk 14:32). The garden of Gethsemane, on the Mount of Olives, takes its name from an olive press that was contained in its plantation. Under the olive branches, Jesus 'often met there with his disciples' (Jn 18:2). We recall another olive branch, at the dawn of the Old Testament, when the dove which Noah had sent out to roam the wilderness of water, bore an olive branch back to the ark in its beak. With it, the dove brought the assurance that the waters were at last subsiding and God was ready to establish a covenant with man. (God's people were to break this covenant. Jeremiah rails against Judah for its apostasy: 'The Lord once called you, "A green olive tree, fair with goodly fruit"; but with the roar of a great tempest he will set fire to it, and its branches will be consumed' [Jer 11:16]).

In the sweetness of the evening, in a stillness broken, perhaps, only by the sound of cicadas, Jesus enters an unimaginable darkness. He begins 'to be greatly distressed and troubled'. And he said to them, 'My soul is very sorrowful, even to death; remain here, and watch' (Mk 14:33, 34). (We hear the haunting rhythm of Psalm 130: 'my soul waits for the Lord more than watchmen for the morning'. But what a grim morning awaits him who set watchmen over Jerusalem, to give Zion rest without fear! [Is 62:6]).

Wholly divine. Wholly human. He sees the torture and degradation that lie ahead and prays with all his heart that this hour might pass from him. But the horror he endures is worse even than the contemplation of his own terrible death: 'For our sake he made him to be sin who knew no sin' (2 Cor 5:21). Or, in the words of Isaiah: 'Surely he has borne our griefs and carried our sorrows ... the Lord has laid on him the iniquity of us all' (Is 53:4, 6).

Utterly sinless, Jesus, in some terrible way, exposes himself to the most malignant evil. He offers himself as a bearer of all sin so that, through his atonement, all sin can be capable of being forgiven. We can dimly imagine how his soul reaches backwards and forwards through the millennia, contemplating – no, far more than that, experiencing – unspeakable cruelty and wickedness in a world where rejection of God produced and produces continuing crucifixions. He takes upon himself the searing pain of the victim and the black weight of remorse that the sinner should experience, but does not. He takes upon himself the immense sorrow that man – created in God's image and, in that primeval garden, given dominion over all the loveliness of the created world – should have become so monstrously distorted through his refusal to love. Man, created for love and joy, turns so easily to hatred and misery.

The foul weight literally crushes him to the ground. The pitiable cry rings out: 'My Father, if it be possible, let this cup pass from me' (Mt 26:39).

Three times in his terrible distress, he comes to them, and each time he finds them sleeping 'for their eyes were very heavy; and they did not know what to answer him' (Mk 14:40). Do Solomon's words ring down the centuries: 'When will you arise from your sleep?' (Prov 6:9). He turns away from them, he of whom the psalmist wrote, 'He who keeps Israel will neither slumber nor sleep' (Ps 121:4).

If there is one word that springs to mind about the apostles during these crucial hours, it is 'apathy'. The word means 'not suffering'. The disciples mentally withdraw from the suffering Christ in that quiet garden. Shortly, as the final act of his passion moves towards its great and terrible conclusion, they will withdraw even their physical presence. But apathy can be shaken off, and the disciples will later atone for their abandonment. Ten of the Eleven will pay the ultimate price for the witness they will bear to him.

Alone, Jesus is fighting an exhausting battle within himself against the natural desire to avoid suffering. Slowly, he yields to the will of the Father: 'My Father, if this cannot pass until I drink it, thy will be done' (Mt 26:42). 'Thy will be done.' The same acceptance with which his mother agreed to bring him into the world: 'I am the handmaid of the Lord; let it be to me according to your word.' Jesus, with obedience as willing as Mary's, accepts the cup of salvation. Resolution follows conflict (and we should remember that the word 'agony' literally means 'contest'); just as Psalm 116 moves from the despair of 'The snares of death encompassed me; the pangs of Sheol laid hold on me' to a ringing note of deliverance: 'I kept my faith, even when I said, "I am greatly afflicted" … I will lift up the cup of salvation.' This is

Jesus, Mary's son: 'I am thy servant, the son of thy handmaid' (Ps 116:16).

Mary moved from obedience to exultation. The obedience of Jesus is also a willed obedience, which brings with it its own courage and fortitude. This is no passive submission to God's will; it is an active desire to accomplish what God wants. It is a realisation that his kingdom cannot come unless his will is done.

Jesus, his battle won, does not sit and wait for his tormentors. He has drunk the Father's cup to the dregs and it has fortified him. Charged with energy, he goes forward to embrace his destiny. Torches are flickering among the trees; there is the tramp of military feet, the clink of swords, the rising clamour of a hostile crowd. 'Rise,' he urges the apostles, 'let us be going; see, my betrayer is at hand' (Mt 26:46). His resolve will not weaken again. But his voice surely breaks when he says 'Friend, why are you here?' (Mt 26:50), as Judas lays his cheek against Jesus' cheek in that most treacherous kiss.

Prayer

'Could you not watch one hour with me?' Words from your agony that haunt with their reproach. Words that are so often so applicable to me, Lord. How often I find excuses to be doing something, rather than being with you in prayer. Ten minutes is often too much time to find – let alone an hour.

And yet, it is in prayer that I can fully be. What is it, then, that so constantly draws me away? What is it that makes me want to fill my day with activity, to escape from my present, my here and now? What is it that makes me seek satisfaction in the arid, while a well of living water is there, at the very centre of myself, waiting to be tapped?

Perhaps, if I am honest, it is that so much of my prayer is simply unrewarding. I seem to sit at the edge of that well, and my prayers disappear over its edge, but there is no stirring in the water, no answering echo from its depths. Discouraged almost as soon as I begin, I look outward again and extraneous thoughts come flooding in. But somewhere inside me I recognise that the 'outside' is actually within me. In my soul resides he whom Teilhard de Chardin describes as the centre of centres upholding the universe. And I, with the glory of the universe lying at my centre, am too blind and too lazy to reach into it.

'Thy will be done.' It is the hardest prayer of all to say with sincerity and I have to remind myself that the more I can pray it, the more I will come to mean it. And, in one of the many seeming contradictions of scripture, obedience will set me free – free from apathy and a sense of futility, free from devouring anxiety and crippling fear.

Lord, help me to realise that prayer is not a state I can drop into at will. Over and over again, you urged the disciples to 'watch and pray'. 'And what I say to you I say to all: Watch' (Mk 13:37). Watch, stay awake, be alert. Help me not to deaden myself with the transitory and illusory. Help me truly to watch and pray.

Second Sorrowful Mystery:
The Scourging at the Pillar

From Pillar of Cloud to Pilate's Court

'Then all the disciples forsook him and fled' (Mt 26:56). After a brief, clumsy confrontation, their courage deserts the disciples and they leave Jesus alone with the forces of darkness. Peter follows at a distance, but his abandonment will be even greater, his denial more compete.

Now comes the travesty of justice, as Jesus is brought before a hastily assembled council of the Sanhedrin. The population of Jerusalem has tripled for the feast; many of Jesus' followers are here. The priests are desperate to have Jesus dispatched before the people can rally around him. Also, if they are to succeed in having him sentenced to execution, that execution must take place before the feast begins.

The assembly is presided over by the high priest, Caiaphas, who set the machinery in place for Jesus' downfall at the time of the raising of Lazarus from the dead. This is a man governed by expediency; he kept a cool head as panic mounted among his peers: 'What are we to do? ... If we let him go on thus, every one will believe in him, and the Romans will come and destroy both our holy place and our nation.' We can almost hear the contempt in his voice as he responds: 'You know nothing at all; you do not understand that it is expedient for you that one man should die for the people, and that the whole nation should not perish' (Jn 11:47-9). This is a man unlikely to be troubled with scruples. His moment has come. He has no moral problems about stacking the prosecution with perjurers.

In the flickering torchlight, the Supreme Judge faces the human accuser. 'Yet he opened not his mouth; like a lamb that is led to the slaughter, and like a sheep that before his shearers is

47

dumb, so he opened not his mouth' (Is 53:7). The false witnesses
have their day: are any of them troubled by the long echo from
Sinai: 'You shall not follow a multitude to do evil; nor shall you
bear witness in a suit, turning aside after a multitude, so as to
pervert justice' (Ex 23:2)? These were among the words spoken
to Moses from 'the thick darkness where God was' (Ex 20:21).
Shortly after, Israel's acceptance of the covenant with God was
sealed by blood. Now, the blood that will seal the new covenant
is soon to be shed.

The testimony is transparently contradictory: 'We have made
a covenant with death, and with Sheol we have an agreement;
when the overwhelming scourge passes through it will not
come to us, for we have made lies our refuge, and in falsehood
we have taken shelter' (Is 28:15). It is increasingly difficult for
Caiaphas to secure an agreement to bring Jesus before Pilate,
who alone has the authority to carry out a death sentence. Time
is critical: Caiaphas needs Jesus condemned and executed before
the crowds of his supporters have an opportunity to rally. Jesus
remains silent despite repeated requests from Caiaphas to respond to the allegations of the witnesses. Finally, Caiaphas is
goaded beyond endurance by the silence of Jesus. He rises from
his seat (in these hearings, the prisoner stood before his seated
accusers) and hurls the question across the shadowy chamber:
'Are you the Christ, the Son of the Blessed?'

Jesus' words ring out at last, resounding, unequivocal: 'I am;
and you will see the Son of Man seated at the right hand of
Power, and coming with the clouds of heaven' (Mk 14:61, 62).
Do the minds of some of the Sanhedrin, so well versed in the
scriptures, drift back to the vision of Daniel: 'and behold, with
the clouds of heaven, there came one like a son of man' (Dan
7:13)? Or are they all overcome with indignation at what ap-
pears to them the most blatant blasphemy?

For Caiaphas, the waiting is over. Jesus has himself presented
him with all the evidence he needs. Caiaphas, with calculated
drama, rends his garments in a gesture of grief and pain as old
as Genesis: with this same dramatic gesture Jacob greeted the

false news of Joseph's death; with this same action, David mourned Jonathan.

The members of the Sanhedrin respond instantly to the emotive action of Caiaphas. Condemning him as deserving to die, they rain Jesus with insults, blows and spittle. The guards into whose hands he is delivered share in the orgy of loathing as they, in turn, 'received him with blows' (Mk 14:65).

At some point in the nightmare of this evening, Jesus, being dragged through the courtyard of the high priest's house, comes face to face with Peter. The short burst of courage that led Peter, finally, to follow the arrested Jesus has evaporated. The words of his third, emphatic, denial of Jesus have just left his lips when 'the Lord turned and looked at Peter' (Lk 22:61). The denial, as described by Mark, could not have been more grievous: Peter, sick with terror, invokes curses on himself as he speaks – in other words, he invokes God himself. What a moment for Jesus! The betrayal by Judas was not entirely unexpected – the warning signs were there from early on. But Peter, the rock on which Jesus said he would build his church! Did his mind flash back to the aftermath of the feeding of the four thousand, and the glory of his own passionate assertion: 'You are the Christ, the Son of the Living God' (Mt 16:16)?

How infinitely lonely a moment for Jesus, and how infinitely terrible for Peter. No wonder his eyes fall before what must have been an indescribable look of sorrow and reproach. 'And he went out and wept bitterly' (Lk 22:62).

Perhaps, at that very moment, Judas is knotting the rope around his neck in the ultimate act of despair. Remorse can kill, or can purify. Judas goes into unimaginable darkness; Peter will go on to be a blazing witness to Christ. His courage will never falter again and will win for him the crown of martyrdom.

The dreadful night moves into dawn and, with it, another trial, this time in the praetorium before Pontius Pilate. Christ's own prophecy is fulfilled: 'he will be delivered to the Gentiles' (Lk 18:32). The Jews cannot enter, for fear of defilement, so Pilate comes out to meet them. The charge has now been changed from blasphemy – which was unlikely to interest Pilate – to sedition: 'We found this man perverting our nation, and forbidding us to give tribute to Caesar, and saying that he himself is Christ a king' (Lk 23:2).

Pilate grasps at all possible opportunities to rid himself of this disturbing problem. He, even more than Caiaphas, is alive to the extreme volatility of the situation in Jerusalem. There are about 100,000 people in the city; Jerusalem at this time is a lighted keg, ready to explode at any moment. The last thing he wants is a riot. He offers to release Jesus in place of Barabbas, eventually sending Jesus to Herod. But Herod is as disconcerted by Jesus as was Pilate: hoping for some sensation, he is thrown by his prisoner's silence and resorts to mockery – dressing Jesus in gorgeous apparel and inviting his soldiers to join in ridiculing him. Mockery as a reaction to disappointed expectation – is there any one of us who cannot identify with this response?

The pleasure palling, this tetrarch of Jesus' race sends him back to Pilate. 'I led you on your way in a pillar of cloud, but you led me to Pilate's court': the words of the haunting *Improperiae* of the Good Friday liturgy form a plangent coda to these most sorrowful episodes.

'Then Pilate took Jesus and scourged him'(Jn 19:1). What a horrific scenario lies behind that terse statement. Drained by the terrible agony in the garden, Jesus has been through two trials. It is unlikely he has slept at all during the night. He has been subjected to vicious abuse and is living in the hourly deepening shadow of the cross. Now he is lashed to a pillar and subjected to the cruelty of the Roman *flagrum,* a multi-thonged whip, the thongs often tipped with metal. The image on the Turin Shroud is an unforgettable one: whether the shroud is or is not that of Jesus, its image of a scourging is graphic, with its criss-cross of over a hundred wounds stretching from shoulder to mid-calf, and extending to the front of the body. 'I bore you up with manna in the desert, but you struck me down and scourged me. My people, what have I done to you? How have I offended you? Answer me!'

Prayer

Your path, Lord, from Gethsemane to Pilate's court was marked by the vacillation, prevarication, cowardice and treachery of those who loved you, those who loathed you, and those who were indifferent to you. And I myself, in my relationship with you, have been guilty of all of these base actions, thoughts and words.

It is a sobering thing to note, when contemplating this sorrowful mystery, the uncomfortable resonances. Sobering to see how one can identify not alone with Peter and the fleeing apostles, but with Judas, Herod and Pilate too. Perhaps it's not so disturbing to sympathise with Peter: after all, he went on to redeem his cowardice with ardent courage. But Judas, Lord! How easy to feel guilty beyond forgiveness, to abandon hope, to refuse to feel, to seek the most permanent form of anaesthesia! We do it in smaller ways – by avoiding the suffering of others, by deadening ourselves with distraction. We have been given the indescribable gift of life, and we can so easily go through our days refusing to live.

Have I not also stood in Herod's shoes? So often I look for the sensational, blind to the fact that I live my life in the presence of the divine.

And Pilate – doing all in his power to avoid the inevitable decision. Procrastinating until he can stall no longer – and then ignoring all his obvious reservations in order to make the expedient, the 'sensible' move. When the intangible is weighed up against reality, Pilate knows how the scales must fall. Lord, perhaps our greatest difficulty on this earth is to recognise that our ideas of what is 'real' and 'unreal' are often deeply flawed.

All these treacheries, great and small, have left their mark on my soul, Lord, as the scourge did on your body. That soul, which should be a shining temple of your Spirit, is a shadowed, excoriated dwelling. I might be tempted to abandon it, as Judas sought to do. But I trust you to give me the courage and the tenacity of Peter, that I might put the past resolutely behind and, each day, move forward.

Third Sorrowful Mystery:
The Crowning with Thorns

The King of Glory

Herod returns Jesus to Pilate and to the bitter hostility of the chief priests. It is a savage fulfilment of the Messianic Psalm, Psalm 2: 'The kings of the earth set themselves, and the rulers take counsel together, against the Lord and his anointed' (Ps 2:2).

Herod has clad Jesus in gorgeous apparel. Bruised, sleepless, racked from the agony in the garden, Jesus must look a sorry contrast to the splendour of his clothing. It was Herod's idea of a joke, and the soldiers guarding Jesus clearly appreciate the humour. Having scourged him, they take him back into the praetorium and gather the whole battalion around. 'And they stripped him and put a scarlet robe upon him, and plaiting a crown of thorns they put it on his head, and put a reed in his right hand' (Mt 27:28, 29).

As they place the mockery of a crown on his head, does anyone hear a faint reverberation from Lamentations: 'The crown has fallen from our head; woe to us, for we have sinned!' (Lam 5: 16)? Lamentations mourned the fall of Jerusalem six centuries earlier; some of those present now will live to see it fall again.

Is there nothing in his gaze that can arrest the subsequent monstrous clowning? This suffering man, who has been clad in kingly raiment, and a branch of thorns twisted tightly around his head is, after all, the One foretold in Revelation: 'His eyes are like a flame of fire, and on his head many diadems … He is clad in a robe dipped in blood … he will tread the wine press of the fury of the wrath of God the Almighty' (Rev 19:12-15). But his sacrifice is total. Throughout his passion, he allows nothing to interfere with the suffering inflicted on him. This is the lamb going unprotestingly to slaughter, the sheep dumb before the shearer. This is the Lamb who, enthroned, will be saluted by 'the voice of many angels, numbering myriads of myriads and thousands of thousands, saying with a loud voice, "Worthy is the Lamb who was slain, to receive power and wealth and wisdom and might and honour and glory and blessing!"' (Rev 5:11-12).

The soldiers kneel before Jesus and mock him. They beat him about the head, with the reed and with their fists, shouting, 'Hail, King of the Jews!' He is completely friendless, as he was during the night hearing of the Sanhedrin Council.

Pilate makes another effort to avoid executing Jesus. He brings him out to the crowd, dressed in his purple robe and wearing the grotesque crown. Does he hope to evoke pity? Or is he, perhaps, seeking to demonstrate how weak is the charge of sedition? This battered man can hardly be supposed to pose any serious threat to the might of Caesar.

Whatever Pilate's intent, his desired objective is not achieved. The chief priests are beside themselves with rage. They incite the crowd to a frenzy of hatred, screaming for Jesus' crucifixion. Contemptuously, Pilate suggests they take Jesus away themselves and crucify him, since he can find no crime against Jesus. He and the Jews know full well that only the Romans can carry out a crucifixion. In their anger, the Jews move away from the expedient charge of sedition and go to the core of their antagonism: 'We have a law, and by that law he ought to die, because he has made himself the Son of God' (Jn 19:7).

If they thought by this allegation to push Pilate into his decision, the crowd miscalculated. All the superstition of Rome casts its shadow around Pilate: 'When Pilate heard these words, he was the more afraid' (Jn 19:8).

Pilate goes into the praetorium and summons Jesus there. Spiritual and temporal power meet in that strange interview. One senses the growing discomfort of Pilate. He is terrified of being denounced to the Emperor by the chief priests (who will later so forcefully assert their loyalty to Tiberius: 'We have no king but Caesar' [Jn 19:15].) Is he, Pilate the Procurator, going to be seen as less wholeheartedly committed to Rome than the

Emperor's notoriously difficult Jewish subjects? On the other
hand, the extraordinary composure of his prisoner clearly unset-
tles him. Pilate is further disconcerted by the interchange where
he asks Jesus: 'Do you not know that I have power to release
you, and power to crucify you?' and Jesus replies: 'You would
have no power over me unless it had been given you from above
...' (Jn 19:11).

Again, Pilate goes out to the crowd, seeking to set Jesus free.
This time, the chief priests unsheathe their swords: 'If you release this man, you are not Caesar's friend; every one who
makes himself a king sets himself against Caesar' (Jn 19:12). It is
the most forceful argument they can make, and the threat in the
words is barely veiled. This is a time when denunciations to
Rome are a common method of toppling an enemy. Pilate, however, does not yet give in. He sits in the judgement seat and has
Jesus brought before him there. Even now, Pilate receives further tidings to trouble him: 'while he was sitting on the judgement seat, his wife sent word to him, "Have nothing to do with
that righteous man, for I have suffered much over him today in a
dream"' (Mt 27:19).

Perhaps there is another shiver of memory as the word gets
around about the dream of the Procurator's wife. Perhaps older
dreams are remembered, dreams of warning, the dreams of
Pharaoh and Nebuchadnezzar ...

'Behold your King! ... Shall I crucify your King?' Back comes
the – to Pilate unanswerable – response: 'We have no king but
Caesar' (Jn 19: 14, 15). Centuries earlier, their ancestors had rejected the theocracy ratified at Sinai, whereby Israel agreed to be
governed by God directly through Moses and subsequently
through the Judges. God told Samuel to accede to their request
to have a king, like all the other nations, but told Samuel to warn
them of what lay in store. Samuel said: "These will be the ways
of the king who will reign over you: he will take your sons and
appoint them to his chariots ... he will take your daughters to be
perfumers and cooks and bakers ... he will take the best of your
fields and vineyards and olive orchards ... he will take the tenth

of your flocks and you shall be his slaves ... And in that day you will cry out because of your king ... but the Lord will not answer you in that day' (1 Sam 8:11-18).

Nor will the Lord answer on a day yet to come. Those who sought Caesar in preference to Jesus will find they have sown the wind only to reap the whirlwind. There are those in the crowd who will be alive forty years later, to experience the terrible sack of Jerusalem by Rome, when the inhabitants will be starved and then put to the sword and when the temple, the very embodiment of Judaic belief and tradition, will be destroyed utterly.

Pilate can hold out no longer. Even as he makes his fatal decision, he seeks to distance himself from it. 'He took water and washed his hands before the crowd, saying, "I am innocent of this man's blood"' (Mt 27:24).

Pilate will have been unaware of certain powerful resonances of this gesture and these words, but many of his audience will not. The chief priests, so thoroughly versed in the law, will surely remember a particular law outlined in Deuteronomy. It concerns sacrifice to atone for murder. A heifer must be slain and 'all the elders of that city nearest to the slain man shall wash their hands over the heifer ... and they shall testify, "Our hands did not shed this blood, neither did our eyes see it shed. Forgive, O Lord, thy people Israel, whom thou hast redeemed, and set not the guilt of innocent blood in the midst of thy people"' (Deut 21:7,8).

Any possible uncertainty caused by Pilate's words and symbolic action is short-lived. 'And all the people answered, "His blood be on us and on our children"' (Mt 27:25).

The fate of Jesus is sealed. There he stands, robed in bloodied purple, and crowned with piercing thorn. Again we hear the haunting reproaches of the Good Friday liturgy: 'For you I struck down the kings of Canaan, but you struck my head with a reed. I gave you a royal sceptre, but you gave me a crown of thorns. My people, what have I done to you? How have I have offended you? Answer me!'

Prayer

Jesus, how often have I failed to see the divine under unlikely raiment? Daily I see wonders but am blind to them – like the Israelites in the desert, I often have neither eyes to see nor ears to hear. Within those whom I meet, those whom I dislike, those whom I despise, you dwell – King of Kings and Lord of Lords. Within my own self, too, I fail to find you – perhaps because I do not seek you. Yet you will never be closer to me than in my own soul. I recall Isaiah's warning: 'Seek the Lord while he may be found, call upon him while he is near.'

Lord, help me truly to realise that your majesty is often clothed in strange outer garments. Help me to look below the surface and beyond the hostility and ridicule which may surround your human temples. Help me to realise that you are always near.

Lord, if there is so much in me of the crowd who beheld you and failed to see you, there is also much in me of Pilate. How often have I known the right thing to do and procrastinated endlessly? Have often have I walked away from what was just and necessary that I should do, and then tried in elaborate ways to abrogate responsibility for my inaction? How often, specially, has my course been dictated by fear rather than by hope and love?

Lord, grant that I may perceive with my eyes, hear with my ears, understand with my heart, and turn for you to heal me.

Fourth Sorrowful Mystery:
The Carrying of the Cross

Endurance and Transcendence

'Your enemies shall come fawning to you; and you shall tread upon their high places' (Deut 33:29). These are the last words of Moses. Because of his sin of unbelief and disobedience at Meribah, Moses is not permitted to lead his people into Canaan. However, immediately before his death, the Lord leads him to the top of Mount Pisgah and shows him the Promised Land.

Now Jesus, whom Moses prefigured, is about to mount to a high place and open another Promised Land for all who had been excluded from it by the original sin of Adam. He who will free all enslaved by sin goes to a shameful form of execution reserved for slaves, subversives and criminals. He, whose power transcends any temporal power, is condemned to a death the spectacular cruelty of which is designed to reinforce the notion of the power of the state and the powerlessness of the individual. He will not climb this hill with the 'hind's feet' of the Psalms; this ascent will be a stumbling, painful one. This is the 'mountain of myrrh and the hill of frankincense' (Sol 4:6) – myrrh for burial, frankincense for embalming.

'So they took Jesus, and he went out, bearing his own cross, to the place called the place of a skull, which is called in Hebrew Golgotha' (Jn 19:17). It may have been the crossbeam that Jesus carried, placed across his shoulders and with his arms bound around it; or it may have been the entire cross, laid heavily across one shoulder. Either way, the dragging weight on his torn flesh must impede his progress cruelly.

'Why is thy apparel red, and thy garments like his that treads in the wine press? I have trodden the wine press alone, and from the peoples no one was with me' (Is 63:2-3). Deserted by most of his disciples, Jesus is a pitiable figure. Herod's purple robes have been taken from him; he is clad now in his own garments which he had worn after the scourging and which must be stiff with dried blood. The painful crown is twisted around his forehead.

The hostile crowd surges as close to him as the soldiers will permit, howling insults. To the forefront are those who will always take pleasure in another's pain and helplessness. Staggering under his unwieldy burden, Jesus is completely at their mercy. We can too easily imagine the spittle, the punches, the quickly thrust foot which trips him and brings him crashing down on to his unprotected face: 'many were astonished at him – his appearance was so marred, beyond human semblance' (Is 52:14).

Long centuries earlier, Christ's awful sufferings on Calvary are foretold and lamented in the deeply moving Psalm 22. From now until his death, this Psalm will provide a sombre, plangent counterpoint to his escalating suffering: 'But I am a worm, and no man; scorned by men and despised by the people. All who see me mock at me.'

At some point it was feared that, in his terribly weakened state, Jesus might not survive his climb to the cross. So '… they seized one Simon of Cyrene, who was coming in from the country, and laid on him the cross, to carry it behind Jesus' (Lk 23:26). The cross is laid on Simon against his will; indeed, we may assume that he bitterly resents his humiliating burden. Is Jesus – as so many of the sick, the incapacitated, the dependent – painfully aware of the reluctance with which Simon's assistance is given? Already stripped of dignity by his suffering, he must be further humiliated by the obvious distaste with which Simon approaches his task.

However, it is likely that the quality of Christ's acceptance transformed the nature of the giving. We do not know whether Simon was Jew or Gentile; but we do know that his sons, Alexander and Rufus, will become sufficiently prominent in the young Christian church to be mentioned by Mark (Mk 15:21). Was Simon's involuntary sharing of Christ's suffering, then, a transforming experience? Did he, on accepting Jesus' yoke, find, after all, that the yoke was easy and the burden light? 'If anyone forces you to go one mile,' Jesus urged at the Sermon on the Mount, 'go with him two miles.' A cross may be imposed by God. It may not be accepted willingly but if, at the end, it is accepted, then comes the grace for going the extra mile.

Not all in that crowd are hostile: among the great multitude of people who follow him are 'women who bewailed and lamented him. But Jesus turning to them said, "Daughters of Jerusalem, do not weep for me, but weep for yourselves and for your children ..."' (Luke 23:28). Before Pilate, the people had cried out: 'His blood be upon us and on our children!' (Mt 27:25). Their words are prophetic, and Jesus foresees the horrific destruction of Jerusalem by the same Romans to whom his own people had delivered him. His words are chilling: 'For behold, the days are coming when they will say, "Blessed are the barren and the wombs that never bore, and the breasts that never gave suck!"' (Luke 23:29). This is a grievous prediction for a people who regard barrenness as an appalling curse.

'Then,' Jesus goes on to say, 'they will begin to say to the mountains, "Fall on us"; and to the hills, "Cover us". For if they do this when the wood is green, what will happen when it is dry?'(Luke 23:31). If the innocent can be put to death so horribly, what will be the lot of the guilty? The Lamb of God is paying the greatest possible price to save his people; but there will be those who choose not to be saved. Jesus may now be referring to the Last Judgement, when people will hide, 'calling to the mountains and rocks, "fall on us and hide us from the face of him who is seated on the throne, and from the wrath of the Lamb"' (Rev 6:16).

Among the crowd there is one woman who does not speak. Mary, the mother of Jesus, is silent as she follows her son to Calvary. Her sorrow transcends weeping and lamentation. It is with infinite courage that she accompanies her son into the darkness. With her silent presence she supports him as he fulfils his terrible vocation. King Solomon, on the day of his wedding, wears 'the crown with which his mother crowned him' (Sol 3:11). Jesus, crowned with thorns and making his painful way along the mountain of myrrh and the hill of frankincense, is about to seal his union with his church, and his mother is there to strengthen him.

Even with Simon of Cyrene helping him, Jesus must be struggling greatly. The ordeal in Gethsemane, the travesty of a trial, the brutal scourging, the savage mockery of the crowning with thorns, have all taken a huge toll. There is no prospect of respite at the end of this cruel journey; an agonising death awaits. 'I am poured out like water, and all my bones are out of joint; my heart is like wax, it is melted within my breast; my strength is dried up …' (Ps 22:14, 15).

Jesus, throughout his public life, has gone to high places to pray. We are often told how he withdrew to the hills. It was on a mountain that he wrestled with Satan, preached the Sermon on the Mount, wrought the miracle of the loaves and fishes, was transfigured. Now he arrives on Calvary – hill and altar.

On Calvary, there are a few, a very few, familiar faces. Mary, Mary Magdalene, Mary the wife of Clophas, and the beloved apostle. Perhaps he cannot even see them at this point, blinded as he must be by sweat, blood and tears, and thickly surrounded by hostile faces: 'Yea, dogs are round about me; a company of evildoers encircle me' (Ps 22:16).

The torrent of reproach from Good Friday's liturgy surges onward: 'For forty years I led you safely through the desert. I fed you with manna from heaven, and brought you to a land of plenty; but you led your Saviour to the cross. My people, what have I done to you? How have I offended you? Answer me!'

Prayer

Lord, how often have I shouldered your cross unwillingly! You have laid it on my shoulders and I have seen only the burden. I have seldom paused to reflect that, if the woman who touched your garment was instantly healed, how much more powerful might be the sharing of your own cross.

You stumbled up that hill of pain, knowing that there would be no respite when the long climb was over. In the eyes of the few faithful supporters who followed you, this was surely the end. Humiliation heaped on humiliation, and a slave's death waiting. The glory of your entry to Jerusalem a week before must have seemed a cruel illusion. No hope. No escape. You and your faithful all locked together in a spiral of failure, hurt and degradation.

Did you ever despair, Mary, as you followed him into the pit? Or did you numb your feelings and simply endure? And perhaps, at the darkest times, that is all we can do. And perhaps that is in itself a prayer. Lord, sometimes life has lost all its taste; I see no hope of anything better. I will make no pretence of embracing suffering joyfully; I welcome it as little as Simon of Cyrene did. But, in accepting and enduring, you may transform my pain. I may draw strength and hope and life from your cross, as Simon surely did.

Lord, be merciful to me, a sinner.

Fifth Sorrowful Mystery: The Crucifixion

'I will go to the altar of God'

'And they brought him to the place called Golgotha (which means the place of a skull). And they offered him wine mingled with myrrh; but he did not take it. And they crucified him, and divided his garments among them, casting lots for them, to decide what each should take. And it was the third hour when they crucified him' (Mk 15:22-25).

The story, which began with one tree, now culminates on another. The act of pride and disobedience with which Adam and Eve ate the fruit of the Tree of Knowledge is now being expiated. Jesus has been stripped of his clothing, his horrible injuries revealed for the first time to the tormented eyes of his mother. He has been hurled onto the wood of the cross and the soldiers, with the tools of his own trade, have hammered iron through living flesh and blood. Then comes the terrible moment when the cross is raised with its heavy burden, and the nails tear upward through bone and tissue. Insofar as his humanity is concerned, he is being unmade – all dignity has been torn from him and he is exposed on a criminal's cross.

But it seems as though, in the unmaking of his humanity, his divinity emerges more nakedly. His first words from the cross are almost unbelievable. His entire body is one tortured mass which every movement exacerbates; on either side the crucified thieves must be screaming with pain, yet his words are of forgiveness: 'Father, forgive them; for they know not what they do' (Lk 23:34). And his next words, spoken to the penitent thief, are confident beyond all probability: 'Truly, I say to you, today you will be with me in Paradise' (Lk 23:43). Can anyone have seemed less likely to make a deathbed conversion than that poor criminal, and can there be any greater proof that the Lord is listening for our voice until literally the last seconds of our lives?

And is there a message here, too, about the redemptive value of suffering? Suffering can dehumanise, or it can be transformed into something that regenerates, remakes. In the repentant thief's case, he converted his own suffering into a key that in the closing breaths of his life unlocked the gates to heaven. A sinner will accompany Jesus, who came to heal sinners, as he opens the gates of paradise.

Paradise still seems a long way off for those at the foot of the cross. For John, for Salome the mother of James and John, Mary the wife of Clophas, and Mary Magdalene, all must have seemed lost by now. For poor Salome, especially, who had asked that her sons might sit, one at his right hand and one at his left, when he came into his kingdom, his dying words to the thief must ring especially hollow. But still, they are there – whether from love, from loyalty, or from pity, is not important. And perhaps we have a lesson the learn here too: perhaps it is enough, at times, simply to place ourselves in the presence of the Lord, no matter how disenchanted, how discouraged or how distant from him we may feel: 'By your endurance you will gain your lives' (Lk 21:19). We should remember that, having endured on Calvary, these same women will be the first to uncover the glory of the resurrection.

There is one person at the foot of the cross at whose feelings we cannot guess. This is Mary. She remains silent – indeed, no words of hers have been recorded since she urged the servants at the wedding feast of Cana: 'Do whatever he tells you' (Jn 2:5). This is the woman prone to pondering things in her heart, as she did when Simeon uttered his chilling prophecy in the temple so many years before. This is the woman who needs no reminder from the psalmist to 'Be still, and know that I am God' (Ps 46:10).

God, but man too. Man, capable of fear and pain, just as was the child she raised and with whose hurts and sorrows she had a mother's intimate familiarity. Does she see again in his gaze from the cross the mute appeal of the child whom she has nursed through the various troubles of childhood? Is the sword of which Simeon spoke twisting in the core of her heart now that he is so utterly beyond all her mother's power to comfort and heal?

Her very presence at the cross is courage beyond imagining. She has chosen to be with him to the end, to witness the full extent of his pain. Hers will probably be the last human face on which he will look with recognition and love, just as it was the first. She will cradle his mutilated dead body as once she cradled his perfect little one. 'Is it nothing to you, all who pass by? Look and see if there is any sorrow like my sorrow …' (Lam 1:12).

As her thoughts are with him, his are with her now. Seeing her and the beloved disciple, he says: 'Woman, behold, your son!' Then he said to the disciple, 'behold, your mother!' And from that hour the disciple took her to his own home' (Jn 19:26,27). Through her, he came into the world. In leaving the world, he gives her back to the human race as universal mother – faithful, loving, courageous, and an enduring link with him.

The sky suddenly darkens, a darkness that will last until the Lord's death. The blackness seems to be echoed in his next words: 'Eloi, Eloi, lama sabachtani?' which means 'My God, my God, why has thou forsaken me?' (Mk 15:34). The cry is made in a loud voice – is it a cry of despair, as is often believed, or a cry of triumph? It would be understandable that Jesus might falter, however briefly. To the soldiers at his feet, busy dicing for his clothes, the words would be taken at face value. But if we look more closely at the words, we could take another view. These are the opening words of Psalm 22, that powerful song of desolation. Every pious Jew would have known this psalm, line for line. The chief priests, scribes and elders gathered below him must be stopped dead in their tracks – they who, a few minutes earlier had wagged their heads at him, saying derisively: 'He trusts in God; let God deliver him now, if he desires him' (Mt 27:43).

'All who see me mock at me,' says the psalm, 'they make mouths at me, they wag their heads; "He committed his cause to the Lord; let him deliver him, let him rescue him, for he delights in him!"'

Does a stillness fall upon the crowd, broken only by the rattling of the dice? '… they have pierced my hand and feet … they divide my garments among them; and for my raiment they cast lots.'

Do their minds race ahead to the prayer for deliverance that comes next in the psalm: 'But thou, O Lord, be not far off!' Is it at this point they begin – derisively? a little uncertainly? – to mutter, 'Wait, let us see whether Elijah will come to save him' (Mt 27:49). The ringing conclusion of the psalm is a long way removed from the despair of the opening: 'men shall tell of the Lord to the coming generation, and proclaim his deliverance to a people yet unborn'. The words may be at once a warning to the hostile, and a comfort to the faithful. He has nearly done.

'I thirst' (Jn 19:28). They put vinegar on a sponge and, on a long stick, bring the sponge to his lips. Do they pause again and remember words from another of the great messianic psalms: '… for my thirst they gave me vinegar to drink' (Ps 69:21)?

The immense sacrifice is reaching its climax. Priest and victim, he completes his mission on earth. On that gruesome altar, he executes the very act of atonement. The breach with God, begun with Adam and Eve, is now healed by the new Adam. 'It is finished' (Jn 19:30). The first creation was described in similar words in Genesis: 'And on the seventh day God finished his work which he had done …' (Gen 2:2). Christ has now finished the work with which the new creation is starting. It is surely a cry of exultation.

Now, he can finally go to the Father. There is no ambivalence, no lack of confidence in his dying words. 'Father, into thy hands I commit my spirit!' (Lk 23:46). His closing words yet again evoke the psalms – appropriately, a psalm of deliverance: 'Into thy hand I commit my spirit; thou hast redeemed me, O Lord, faithful God' (Ps 31:5).

Prayer

Lord, who is there that walks this life without a cross on their shoulders? Sometimes it is light; sometimes so heavy it thrusts heart and soul and mind to the ground. They say you are closest to us in times of suffering – but it is also at those times that you can seem most distant. How often has life seemed to me a barren landscape, across which I move painfully, dragged down by suffering or weighted by sorrow, my wandering aimless, the landscape featureless, unpeopled, unlit? Your presence, sometimes experienced so strongly, sometimes so remote that I doubt I ever experienced it. Where do I find within myself the courage to transform this suffering into something regenerative? That mustard seed of faith, planted within me before time began, seems to have atrophied within me through lack of nurture …

Sometimes, I hurl the words into the empty landscape: 'Father, Father, why hast thou forsaken me?' And sometimes, some precious times, your grace passes in to me and I rise, slowly but certainly, into the light. Once again I can say, 'Thou hast redeemed me, O Lord, faithful God'.

The Glorious Mysteries

First Glorious Mystery: The Resurrection

From Fall to Redemption

He is taken down from the cross and Mary holds his bloodied body in her arms. Nicodemus arrives, bearing his gift of myrrh and aloes, a hundred pounds' weight. 'Your robes are all fragrant with myrrh and aloes ...' wrote the psalmist, describing the wedding of the king. The King, wedded now to his church, lies in his shroud. Does Mary remember that long ago gift of myrrh, received from the Magi in Bethlehem? Does she recall how she held him closely in her arms then, too – in all the new wonder of an extraordinary motherhood?

She must surely recall Bethlehem for another reason, too. The leaden skies – the sun's light has failed for the past three hours – are darkening further. The body must be buried before night, but there is nowhere to place It. A stranger came to the rescue in Bethlehem; Joseph of Arimathea comes now, at the critical moment, having obtained permission from Pilate to take away the body: 'Now in the place where he was crucified there was a garden, and in the garden a new tomb where no one had ever been laid' (Jn 19:41).

The great sweep from fall to redemption starts and comes to completion in a garden. Redemption must seem a long way off in the terrible aftermath of Good Friday's brutality. The disciples have virtually all fled. The handful of faithful women remain to perform a sad task: they bind his corpse with the spices; later they will prepare spices and ointments for a full embalming, to take place when the Sabbath is over. All these actions suggest finality. There is no expectation of resurrection here.

Yet, even now, the dead Christ calls forth a witnessing, just as he did in his dying moments on the cross. The crucified thief

made his extraordinary prayer when all hope seemed dead;
now, when Jesus himself is dead, Nicodemus and Joseph
emerge from darkness – literally in the case of Nicodemus: 'who
had at first come to him by night' (Jn 19:39). And Joseph was 'a
disciple of Jesus, but secretly, for fear of the Jews' (Jn 19:38).
Why do these two cautious men choose now, of all times, to de-
clare their discipleship? Is the clue to be found in Luke's words
about Joseph: 'he was looking for the kingdom of God' (Lk
23:51)? If so, then their faith is even more remarkable than that of
the repentant thief: Jesus was at least alive when the thief made
his prayer.

The sorrowful little procession takes place to the garden
tomb, augmented by an armed guard: it is the Pharisees, rather
than the disciples, who remember the words of Jesus 'After
three days I will rise again' (Mt 27:63). The great stone is rolled
against the entrance, and the guards see to it that the tomb is
sealed. Good Friday moves into Holy Saturday, the most silent
day of the church's year. Jesus is among the dead: in the ancient
words of the Creed: 'He descended into hell.'

'And when the Sabbath was past, Mary Magdalene, and
Mary the mother of James, and Salome, bought spices, so that
they might go and anoint him. And very early on the first day of
the week they went to the tomb when the sun was risen' (Mk 16:
1-2).

We can picture the women on their sorrowful mission. They
move through the garden with heavy hearts, concentrated on
the grim task that lies ahead of them, oblivious to all the sights
and sounds and smells of the dawning spring morning. They are
oblivious, above all, to the glorious presence of the risen Christ
not a stone's throw away from them.

Their great concern is how they are going to roll back the
heavy stone that seals the tomb – 'it was very large' (Mk 16:4).
Then they arrive at the tomb to find the stone rolled back, and an
angel of the Lord seated upon it: 'His appearance was like light-
ning, and his raiment white as snow' (Mt 28:3). The angel, or angels (Luke and John mention two), are alone in the tomb: there is

no body. Only the linen winding cloths remain and, neatly rolled up, the napkin that covered the face.

'Why do you seek the living among the dead?' the angels ask. Then, in view of the women's evident incomprehension, they go on to prompt: 'Remember how he told you, while he was still in Galilee, that the Son of Man must be delivered into the hands of sinful men, and be crucified, and on the third day rise.' There is still no evidence that the women understand what is being said to them and, when they go to the apostles with the story, 'these words seem to them an idle tale, and they did not believe them' (Lk 24: 4-11).

It seems extraordinary to us that these followers of Jesus could have been so deaf to the meaning of his words. Many of them had, after all, witnessed his dominion over death when he recalled from the dead the widow's son at Nain, and the daughter of Jairus. More recently still, just a few days earlier in fact, there had been the powerful and immensely moving episode at Bethany. 'Lord, if you had been here, my brother would not have died', Mary of Bethany said to Jesus in heartbroken reproach. 'Your brother will rise again,' Jesus told her, and Martha failed to take the words literally. 'I am the resurrection and the life,' Jesus went on, and then, 'deeply moved in spirit and troubled', he called for the stone to be removed from the tomb. Martha and the other onlookers still did not understand: 'Lord, by this time there will be an odour, for he has been dead four days.' Then Jesus replied, in words that must surely have sent a thrill through all who listened: 'Did I not tell you that if you would believe you would see the glory of God?' And he summoned Lazarus forth (Jn 11: 21-43).

Mary Magdalene, out of whom he cast seven devils, has as little expectation of the resurrection as any of the other followers. Weeping, she stoops to look into the tomb and sees the angels, who ask her why she is weeping. 'Because they have taken away my Lord, and I do not know where they have laid him' (Jn 20:13). Blind with tears, she turns around and sees a man whom she takes to be the gardener: 'Sir, if you have carried him away, tell me where you have laid him, and I will take him away'.

'Mary'. He calls her by name and she recognises him. 'I have called you by name, you are mine', Isaiah wrote, describing God's redeeming love (Is 43:1). Mary had herself experienced that redemption. It is immensely significant that she is the first person he chooses to meet in his risen glory. 'Mary': this is the Good Shepherd, who said of himself: 'the sheep hear his voice, and he calls his own sheep by name and leads them out' (Jn 10:3). As he called Lazarus back from literal death. As he called Mary out from spiritual death. As he calls us. Here is the Good Shepherd who has laid down his life for his sheep of his own free will, just as he can take that life back again. Does Mary remember those words: 'No one takes it from me, but I lay it down of my own accord. I have power to lay it down, and I have power to take it again'? (Jn 10:18).

Mary falls at his feet and worships Jesus. In this Easter dawn, the Messiah stands before her, the eternal Priest, come from 'the womb of the morning … a priest for ever after the order of Melchizedek' (Ps 110:4). This is the Light of the World who has triumphed over darkness: 'The light shines in the darkness, and the darkness has not overcome it' (Jn 1:5). This is 'the root and the offspring of David, the bright morning star' (Rev 22:16) – celebrated in the *Exsultet* of the Easter Vigil as 'Christ, that Morning Star, who came back from the dead, and shed his peaceful light on all mankind, your Son who lives and reigns for ever and ever'.

Prayer

Lord, help me to realise that when I am weighed down with sorrow, anxiety or hopelessness, you are no further from me than you were to the women in that dawn garden. Sadness and pain can blind me to the fact that your healing presence is beside me, can make me deaf to your voice calling me by name. 'I have called you by name and you are mine.'

How I can identify with Mary and the other women! I, too, have heard your words and did not understand. I have seen and did not perceive. I have experienced your redemptive love in

my own past, and failed to remember it. Wrapped in sorrow, I
have passed you in my daily life without recognising you. I have
trodden a dark and lonely path, oblivious to your glory shining
around me. I have made of my life a wasteland of unnecessary
worry, when you have already removed the seemingly immov-
able obstacles that trouble me.

Lord, I too have sought you too often among dead things.

When I am entombed in hopelessness, grant that I may hear
your voice, as Lazarus did. Let me hear those blessed words you
uttered at Lazarus' grave: 'Unbind him, and let him go.'

Second Glorious Mystery: The Ascension

Love Ascending

Jesus said to Mary Magdalene: 'Do not hold me, for I have not yet ascended to the Father; but go to my brethren and say to them, I am ascending to my Father and your Father, to my God and your God' (Jn 20:17).

We can hear, in his words to Mary Magdalene, his immense concentration on this ascension. He has never been anything but centred upon the Father; now his return to the Father is imminent. The yearning is about to be replaced with fulfilment. 'I came from the Father and have come into the world; again, I am leaving the world and going to the Father' (Jn 16:28). He is about to be glorified in the presence of the Father, 'with the glory which I had with thee before the world was made' (Jn 17:5).

But in ascending to the Father, he is also conscious that his disciples will see him no more in this world. His work is not quite done.

'That very day two of them were going to a village named Emmaus ... and talking with each other about all these things that had happened. While they were talking and discussing together, Jesus himself drew near and went with them ... And they stood still, looking sad' (Lk 24:13-17). As Mary, also heartbroken, failed to recognise the risen Christ, so too do Cleopas and his companion fail. It is a moving and wholly understandable episode. The high hopes of these disciples have been shattered: '... we had hoped he was the one to redeem Israel.' They refer, with thinly disguised scepticism, to the women's story of the angels and the empty tomb. They have no more expectation of the resurrection than did the apostles; they have no understanding of what redemption might truly mean. They wanted kingship and triumph; the glory of Palm Sunday turned to ashes for them on Good Friday, as he on whom they had pinned their hopes died a slave's death. They have hoped for what was circumscribed and temporal; they have not yet been 'born anew to a living hope' (1 Peter 1:3). Unless they see, they cannot believe: 'Some of those who were with us went to the tomb, and found it just as the women had said; but him they did not see' (Lk 24:24).

'O foolish men, and slow of heart to believe all that the prophets have spoken!' cries Jesus. And then, patiently, gently, he takes them on a journey through the prophets, starting with Moses, and interpreting all the passages concerning himself. It must have been an extraordinary narrative. There were so many prefigurings of him: the redemptive Lamb without blemish, slaughtered at the first Passover; Isaac, the beloved son, whom Abraham was ready to sacrifice; the great High Priests, Aaron and Melchizedek; Joshua, leading the people of God into the Promised Land and interceding for them when, as so often, they went astray; David, the great Shepherd-King.

And no wonder their hearts burned within them when he recited as he must surely have done, the 22nd Psalm, which opens with his own words from the cross: 'My God, my God, why has thou forsaken me?' and which goes on to depict so graphically the horrors of crucifixion. And the imagery of Isaiah's 53rd chapter must sear their consciousness: 'a man of sorrows', a 'lamb led to the slaughter', one 'numbered with the transgressors' ... When he comes to the penultimate book of the Old Testament, that of the prophet Zechariah, how the words must resonate with their own sorrow: '... when they look on him whom they have pierced, they shall mourn for him, as one mourns for an only child, and weep bitterly over him ...' (Zech 12:10).

The disciples are deeply affected, but still – like Mary at the tomb – they fail to recognise him. His face may well be transfigured by his closeness to the Father. It takes the blessing and breaking of the bread to open their eyes. The apostles can hardly have failed to tell about the breaking of the bread at the Last

Supper – broken as his body was to be broken, and the wine poured as his blood would be poured – and how he urged them to commemorate him thereafter in the breaking of bread. It is significant that in this sacrament he is at last revealed to them, as he was not when he walked and talked beside them.

Some days later, he will again break bread – this time by the Sea of Tiberias. The followers of Jesus will need no further prompting to celebrate the eucharist, knowing that 'as often as you eat this bread and drink the cup, you proclaim the Lord's death until he comes' (1 Cor 11:26).

Cleopas and the other disciple saw, and did not know that they saw. The apostles see Jesus on the evening of the same day, and suppose they are looking at a ghost. 'Why are you troubled, and why do questionings rise in your heart?' asks Jesus, 'See my hands and feet, that it is I myself; handle me, and see ...' (Lk 24:39). John will later write of 'that which we have heard, which we have seen with our eyes, which we have looked upon and touched with our hands' (1 Jn 1:1). Thomas will place his hands in the wounds of Jesus, and the experience will draw from him the ringing affirmation of Christ's divinity: 'My Lord and my God!' Fully human, and fully divine. Eternally human, eternally divine. His human nature is glorified, just as his divinity is humanised. Our human nature will be forever in him; his divinity dwells within us, and will remain with us even to the consummation of the world.

Now, the disciples both see and believe. More blessed still, says Jesus, are those who do not see and yet believe. Jesus is conscious that his time to leave them is almost at hand. Soon, there will be a time when no one alive will have seen him. It is time for the emphasis to switch from seeing to hearing. In the generations to follow, the belief of Christ's followers will be founded on the testimony of the apostles – on what they hear, rather than on what they see: 'he who hears you hears me' (Lk 10:16). His word, after all, will endure forever, and 'if you continue in my word, you are truly my disciples, and you will know the truth, and the truth will make you free' (Jn 8:31, 32). Did he, in his discussion of Moses and the prophets on the road to Emmaus, remind the disciples of Moses' admonition that 'the word is very near you; it is in your mouth and in your heart' (Deut 30:14)?

The God of the Old Testament appointed his great shepherd-king, David. Now, there remains another task for the Good Shepherd: to appoint an earthly shepherd in his place. The material can scarcely have seemed promising: an utter failure to comprehend the possibility of the resurrection was preceded by an ignominious show of cowardice at Calvary. Peter, so extravagant in all his protestations of love and fidelity, could hardly have reneged more abjectly. It is easy to imagine his self-loathing as he stands by the Risen Lord after the symbolic catch of fish at the Sea of Tiberias. Jesus turns to him and elicits from Peter a triple affirmation of love to parallel the three terrible denials. With one exception, the apostles' courage was cruelly lacking in the final hours of Jesus; 'Feed my lambs', Simon Peter is instructed, 'feed my sheep'. Jesus has chosen his shepherd from among the fallen. The Redeemer has indeed redeemed!

The time has come for him to leave. He summons them to a mountain near Bethany, most probably Mount Olivet. What memories there must be for all of them as they come into Bethany: 'Did I not tell you that if you would believe you would see the glory of God?', as he led Lazarus forth from the dead (Jn 11: 21-43). Now, that glory is about to be his. Just as his earthly nature is about to be in heaven, so, too, heaven is now upon earth.

Urging the apostles to remain in Jerusalem 'until you are clothed with power from on high' (Lk 24:49), he brings them to a high mountain. While he blesses them, he parts from them and ascends to the right hand of God. 'I came from the Father and have come into the world; again, I am leaving the world and going to the Father' (Jn 16:28).

Prayer

Lord, do I really believe that you lived on earth, died and arose to everlasting life? If I did, surely I would be more able to recognise you in the hearts of others, in scripture, in the sacraments? But, surrounded as I am with your presence, I am often as unable to recognise it, as were Cleopas and his companion. Unable, because like them, like the apostles, too, I am so often not expecting to find it. To Cleopas and his friend the revelation came after long listening. I know I do not listen enough. I besiege you with words, but I do not wait for a response. Perhaps, in my heart of hearts, I do not expect a response. Lord, strengthen my faith – that faith which will give me eyes that see, and ears that hear; that faith which will reveal your luminous presence at the very heart of myself.

Then, I may begin the long ascent. And I remind myself that, for you, without the descent among the dead there could have been no ascension. Without Good Friday, there could have been no Easter Sunday.

Lord, grant that one day I may go where you are, and behold the glory the Father gave you before the foundation of the world.

Third Glorious Mystery:
The Descent of the Holy Spirit

Life Descending

Fifty days have passed since the resurrection. It is the feast of Pentecost, which, in the days of the Old Testament, celebrated the first fruits of the harvest. Now, Christ's own harvest is ready for reaping.

Since the ascension, the apostles have been continually in the temple, praising God. From his great discourse at the Last Supper some words, especially, must be generating a sense of joyful expectancy: 'And I will pray the Father, and he will give you another Counsellor, to be with you for ever, even the Sprit of truth … I will not leave you desolate … the Counsellor, the Holy Spirit, whom the Father will send in my name, he will teach you all things' (Jn 14:16-18, 26).

Do they have an inkling now – as certainly Peter will acknowledge later (Acts 2:17-21) – that Jesus is foretelling the fulfilment of Joel's prophecy of 800 years earlier: 'And it shall come to pass afterward, that I will pour out my spirit on all flesh; your sons and your daughters shall prophesy, your old men shall dream dreams, and your young men shall see visions' (Joel 2:28-29)?

They are gathered together in a house in Jerusalem. Perhaps their anticipation is turning to impatience. Perhaps one of them cries out: 'Lord, where is the Counsellor you promised us?' Throughout scripture, God exhorts us to *ask:* 'Ask what I shall give you', the Lord said to Solomon (1 Kings 3:5); 'Ask of me, and I will make the nations your heritage' (Ps 2:8); 'Ask a sign of the Lord your God' (Is 7:11); 'Ask rain from the Lord' (Zech 10:1); 'Ask, and it will be given you' (Mt 7:7). And did the apostles especially remember the words of Jesus at the Last Supper: 'Hitherto, you have asked nothing in my name; ask, and you will receive, that your joy may be full' (Jn 16:24)?

If the apostles did indeed ask in Jesus' name, in that house in Jerusalem, never was prayer more dramatically answered. 'And suddenly a sound came from heaven like the rush of a mighty wind, and it filled all the house where they were sitting. And there appeared to them tongues as of fire, distributed and resting on each one of them. And they were filled with the Holy Spirit and began to talk in other tongues, as the Spirit gave them utterance' (Acts 2:2-4).

This is the baptism in the Spirit and in fire, which Jesus promised at his own baptism in the Jordan. It is an extraordinary event: the mighty blast from heaven filling the room, shaking the very house (as we know from a later manifestation in Acts 4:31). The commencement of the Spirit's indwelling in human hearts is marked in a very physical way: as the great wind enters and fills the hearts and minds and souls of those present, the response is like that of ships under full sail, driven before the Spirit. They are so filled that there can no longer be any fear, any ambivalence, only a raging glory of faith which hurls them into the streets, preaching with joy and an irresistible passion: 'They are filled with new wine', cry some onlookers (Acts 2:13). But this is the 'love ... better than wine' (Sol 1:2), this is the 'joy fulfilled' that Jesus promised in his high priestly prayer at the Last Supper (Jn 17:13). This is the mounting up on eagles' wings foretold by Isaiah (40:31).

The old Adam clothed himself with fig leaves; now his descendants are 'clothed with power from on high' (Lk 24:49). As God breathed life into Adam, the New Adam breathes new life into mankind. This is, in many ways, the Second Coming: God coming into men's hearts, to make his dwelling there; God transfiguring man from within, and creating a transformation so great that all 'were amazed and wondered' (Acts 2:7).

This transforming power is vividly illustrated in one of the readings from the Pentecost liturgy: it is the strange vision of Ezekiel when he is led into the valley of the dry bones. He is ordered by God to call upon 'the breath' to enter the bones, whereupon sinews and flesh and skin are laid upon the bones, 'and the breath came into them, and they lived, and stood upon their feet, an exceedingly great host. Then he said to me, 'Son of man, these bones are the whole house of Israel. Behold, they say, 'our bones are dried up, and our hope is lost; we are clean cut off'. Thus says the Lord God … you shall know that I am the Lord when I open your graves, and raise you from your graves … And I will put my Spirit within you and you shall live.' (Ezek 37:10-14).

It is a new birth and a new baptism. The regenerative power of the Spirit makes it possible for us to become children of God, 'and, if children, then heirs' (Rom 8:17). Without this new birth, we cannot see the kingdom of God (Jn 3:3). With it, we become a new creation, formed by the same Spirit of God which moved over the world in the opening lines of Genesis, when: 'the earth was without form and void, and darkness was upon the face of the deep'.

This new creation is made possible by what Paul, in the letter to Titus, describes as 'the washing of regeneration and renewal in the Holy Spirit' (Tit 3:5). This baptism is not of water, but fire. It is the baptism foretold by John on the banks of the Jordan: 'I baptise you with water for repentance, but he who is coming after me is mightier than I … he will baptise you with the Holy Spirit and with fire'(Mt 3:11). However, it is a fire that ignites rivers of living water in the heart. It is the fulfilment of Isaiah's prophecy: 'With joy you will draw water from the wells of salvation' (Is 12:3).

Fire descended from heaven and consumed Solomon's burnt offerings at the dedication of the temple; fire now descends to mark the opening of a new temple, the temple of the Holy Spirit. As God spoke to Moses from a fire, he will now speak to men from a fire within their hearts. The divinely empowered utterance which was once reserved for the prophets is now available to all men: 'there is in my heart as it were a burning fire shut up in my bones, and I am weary with holding it in, and I cannot' (Jer 20:9).

This fire allows the apostles to proclaim Christ's message to all nations: it spreads from person to person – the fire in each kindling a flame in the next. It is the reversing of the disunity created at Babel. Now there is a new, life-giving unity, and a new universal language – that of divine love.

This is a joy that cannot be contained. It hurls the apostles into the streets, and fires Peter's great Pentecost sermon, with its ringing conclusion: 'Let all the house of Israel therefore know most assuredly that God has made him both Lord and Christ, this Jesus whom you crucified' (Acts 2:36). Three thousand people join the emerging church on that day, 'and the Lord added to their number day by day' (Acts 2:47).

Unless we are born again, we cannot see the kingdom of God. When we are born first, we are born to human life. When we are born 'anew', we receive divine life. 'Truly, truly, I say to you, unless one is born of water and the Spirit, he cannot enter the kingdom of God. That which is born of the flesh is flesh, and that which is born of the Spirit is spirit' (Jn 3:5-6). Without the Spirit, we remain the dry bones of Ezekiel's vision, confined within earthly graves, without hope, without life. As temples of the Spirit, we are 'born anew to a living hope through the resurrection of Jesus Christ from the dead, and to an inheritance which is imperishable, undefiled, and unfading' (1 Pet 1:4). With this rebirth comes certain salvation: 'For I am sure that neither death, nor life, nor angels, nor principalities, nor things present, nor things to come, nor powers, nor height, nor depth, nor anything else in all creation, will be able to separate us from the love of God in Christ Jesus our Lord' (Rom 8:38-39).

Prayer

Oh Lord! I have so often felt that my hope is lost, that I am clean cut off. I lie in my living grave, confined by fear, by apathy, by self. I plod through the outward observance of my religion and it does not touch me. I give so little to it, and I expect so little of it.

What is it that blinds me to the reality of what I read about Pentecost? What makes me refuse to acknowledge that it can happen to me just as it did to the apostles? That within my despised self there is a temple in which your Spirit adores you without ceasing? That, if I go into that temple, I will be freed from my bondage to decay? Is it a fear that, by accepting your greatness at the centre of myself, great things will be asked of me? Is it possible that, in my desire to avoid pain, I also deprive myself of experiencing joy?

Lord, help me find my way into the temple of my own body and baptise me there with the Holy Spirit and with fire. And let me then recognise that fire cannot burn alone; I cannot blaze for long in the isolation of my own soul – my fire cannot live unless it is fuelled by others and kindles others in turn. Help me move out from the darkness of my fearful inertia, and become part of the blaze that was kindled on the first Pentecost. Let me experience the reality of Teilhard de Chardin's words: 'Some day, after we have mastered the winds, the waves, the tides and gravity, man will harness for God the energies of love and then, for the second time in the history of the world, man will discover fire.'[12]

Fourth Glorious Mystery: The Assumption

Ark of the New Covenant

'Is it nothing to you, all who pass by? Look and see if there is any sorrow like my sorrow' (Lam 1:12).

It is Mary's darkest hour. Love and immense courage have brought her to the foot of the cross. Throughout his childhood sufferings, she was there for him. Now she does not flinch from giving all that she is in a position to give – the support of her helpless, loving presence at this bloody execution. Among the many faces below – cruel, mocking, coarse, indifferent – his gaze fixes on hers.

'Woman, behold, your Son!' Then he said to the disciple, 'Behold, your mother!' (Jn 19: 26-27). At the desolate point in Mary's life where her role as a mother seems about to end, it is, instead, suddenly expanded beyond imagining. She is becoming mother not only to the beloved disciple, but to all his kind. While Christ, the new Adam, is in the very act of atoning for the original sin committed in the Garden of Eden, Mary becomes the new Eve, mother of all creation.

When he has gone from her, her new vocation begins. It flowers, not in the full joy of his presence, but in the desert of his absence. In the desert times of our own life, it is good to reflect on this and to remember that all fields need to lie fallow for a time if they are to bear their fullest fruit.

'And from that hour the disciple took her to his own home' (Jn 19:27). We do not know how long Mary remained on earth. She was certainly there in the early days of the church; we know from the Acts of the Apostles that she was accustomed to pray with the disciples, and it is probable that she was present when the Holy Spirit descended in wind and fire at Pentecost.

Life descending, life ascending: it is a theme we meet many times in scripture. We remember Elijah, taken up to heaven by whirlwind and fiery chariot; raised to everlasting life by the God who, in the words of the psalmist, 'makest the clouds thy chariot, who ridest on the wings of the wind, who makes the winds thy messengers, fire and flame thy ministers' (Ps 104:3,4).

The only other person in scripture who was physically raised to eternal life was Enoch, who lived six generations after Adam and of whom we know little, except that he 'walked with God; and he was not, for God took him' (Gen 5:24). Paul elaborates: 'By faith Enoch was taken up so that he should not see death; and he was not found, because God had taken him. Now before he was taken he was attested as having pleased God. And without faith it is impossible to please him' (Heb 11:5, 6).

The belief in Mary's assumption, while not described in scripture, is drawn from the earliest tradition of the church. In the sixth century, Bishop Theoteknos of Livias provided a widely shared rationale in these words: 'It was fitting ... that her all-holy body, her God-bearing body, godlike, undefiled, shining with the divine light and full of glory, should be carried by the apostles in the company of the angels and, after being placed a short time in the earth, should be raised up to heaven in glory with her soul so loved by God ... If he had prepared a place in heaven for the apostles, how much more for his mother; if Enoch had been translated and Elijah had gone to heaven, how much more Mary?'' (*Encomium*, 9).

Mary, like Enoch, has pleased God. And her faith is beyond question: 'blessed is she who believed that there would be a fulfilment of what was spoken to her from the Lord '(Lk 1:45), cries Elizabeth, with her own husband's scepticism uncomfortably fresh in her mind. His disbelief has rendered Zechariah dumb; in contrast, Mary's faith opens her mouth with the glorious and prophetic canticle of the *Magnificat:* 'henceforth, all generations shall call me blessed' (Lk 1:48).

In reflecting on the annunciation, we recalled the prophecy of Malachi, heralding the coming of the Elijah. This prophecy was fulfilled in Mary's womb. In a sense, she became the Ark of the new Covenant, carrying within her the eternal Word of God. The Israelites, wandering in the desert, found direction and safety in following the Ark: '... and the ark of the covenant of the Lord went before them three days journey to seek out a resting place for them. And the cloud of the Lord was over them by day, whenever they set out from the camp' (Num 10:33, 34). When our own journey brings us into the wilderness we can recall the words of Joshua: 'When you see the ark of the covenant of the Lord your God being carried ... then you shall set out from your place and follow it, that you may know the way you shall go, for you have not passed this way before' (Josh 3:3, 4).

Mary, the Ark of the new Covenant, leads us as surely by her example as Moses' Ark led the people of Israel. Her faith, hope and love brought her from the desert of grief and loss into the glory of eternal joy: 'Who is that coming up from the wilderness, leaning upon her beloved?' (Sol 8:5). As the Ark of the Covenant was brought triumphantly into Jerusalem, we can imagine how Mary, at the close of her earthly journey, entered into heavenly glory: 'And they brought the ark of the covenant of the Lord to its place, in the inner sanctuary of the house, in the most holy place, underneath the wings of the cherubim ... the house, the house of the Lord, was filled with a cloud, so that the priests could not stand to minister because of the cloud; for the glory of the Lord filled the house of God' (2 Chr 5: 7, 13-14).

Like the people of Israel, of whom she is often seen as a symbol, Mary has emerged from the desert into great joy. As the Ark is brought into the city of David, it is interesting to recall how David's reaction is not to prostrate himself with fear and trembling. Instead, 'David and all the house of Israel brought up the ark of the Lord with shouting, and with the sound of the horn ...' He is seen by Saul's daughter 'leaping and dancing before the Lord ' (2 Sam 6:15,16). In Chronicles, David's delighted welcoming of the ark to his city is described: 'All Israel brought up the ark of the covenant of the Lord with shouting, to the sound of the horn, trumpets and cymbals, and made loud music on harps and lyres' (1 Chr 15:28). David himself, dressed in fine linen, dances and makes merry before exploding into the psalm of gratitude which rings with confidence, gratitude, hope and love, to which all the people cried 'Amen' (1 Chr 16:8-36).

Mary's life was one immense 'Amen'. At the death of Jesus, Mary became the universal mother. Her assumption is significant for all of us, since it anticipates our own resurrection. If we 'walk with God' as Enoch did, as Mary did, we too can be taken up into glory. Like her, we can anticipate the day when 'this perishable nature must put on the imperishable, and this mortal nature must put on immortality … then shall come to pass the saying that is written: "Death is swallowed up in victory." "O death, where is thy victory? O death, where is thy sting?"' (1 Cor 15:54-5).

Prayer

Lord, scripture so often tells us about the Creator's delight in his people – but we so rarely see the other side of the coin, the creature delighting in his Creator – openly, rapturously, confidently, gaily – the great king performing his ecstatic dance before your altar. Why is David such an alien figure to me? Why can I not identify with him at this moment of triumphant love?

Great though her grief was to be during Christ's passion, Mary's 'Amen' must have brought with it enormous joy over the years in her closeness to him. Why is it that we tend to concentrate mainly on her sorrow: the dark prophecy of Simeon fulfilled on the path to Calvary? When did I ever celebrate my faith as David did? And yet the Ark of the New Covenant is a daily presence in my life, brought into the world by Mary.

John leaped for joy in Elizabeth's womb at the presence of Mary, Ark of the New Covenant. I have been in that presence daily, with no glad quickening of the pulse. I have simply been there, unmoved, indifferent, blind to the glory around me, unwarmed by the boundless and unquenchable love, deaf to the mighty, yet tender, voice that has called me from the beginning of time. Indeed, I have had eyes to see, but saw not, ears to hear, but heard not.

Like the man with the one talent, I have been crippled by fear and inertia, afraid to ask what it is you want of me, lacking the courage to say 'Speak, Lord, your servant is listening'. Lacking, especially, the strength to say 'Do with me what you will'.

At last, I see the possibility of release from this bondage and this darkness. You, who so often healed the paralysed, can heal me now. Your breath can come into me, as it did to the dry bones in Ezekiel's vision, making them live and stand and become an exceedingly great host.

You can release me from death. The words used to describe Israel's release from Egyptian bondage can be as applicable to me as it was to Mary: 'I bore you on eagles' wings and brought you to myself' (Ex 19:4).

Fifth Glorious Mystery: The Coronation

*'When the perishable puts on the imperishable,
and the mortal puts on immortality.'*

She saw her son crowned with thorns; she herself will now be crowned with glory. 'I will make you majestic for ever, a joy from age to age' (Is 60:15). Isaiah is prophesying about the people of Israel during the longed-for period of the messianic reign. However, his words are applicable to Mary too and, through her, to all of us. In Mary's life, we see faith, hope and love forging 'a crown of beauty in the hand of the Lord, and a royal diadem in the hand of your God' (Is 62:3).

We, too, can hope for this crown. Like the foundling child, Israel, we came into the world with nothing. But we share in the promise made to Israel, the hope of rescue from nothingness: 'for like the jewels of a crown they shall shine on his land. Yea, how good and fair it shall be!' (Zech 9:16,17). Like faithless Israel, we have often let the crown go from us 'The joy of our hearts has ceased; our dancing has been turned to mourning. The crown has fallen from our head; woe to us, for we have sinned!' (Lam 5:16).

Mary did not experience the loss of the crown, but her path to it was not won easily. For her, as for us, 'suffering produces endurance, and endurance produces character, and character produces hope, and hope does not disappoint us, because God's love has been poured into our hearts through the Holy Spirit which has been given to us' (Rom 5:3-5). Mary had in abundance the 'endurance and faith of the saints' (Rev 13:10).

It is important to bear in mind how, sometimes, it is enough to endure. To remember Simon of Cyrene on that humiliating journey, where endurance had the power to transform. To remember the endurance of Mary and the other women at the foot of the cross, when all hope seemed dead – those same women who were the first to encounter the radiant splendour of the resurrection. In Christ's own words, 'By your endurance you will gain your lives' (Lk 21:19).

Suffering followed by hope, hope followed by joy, joy followed by endurance – the cycle repeated itself through what we know of Mary's life, culminating in joy. The terrible prophecy of Simeon shadowing the joy of new motherhood; the racking anxiety when the child Jesus was lost in Jerusalem, and the flooding joy of finding him; the later and more grievous loss against the bloody backdrop of Golgotha, and the incandescent hope of the first Easter morning. Her own death and her own resurrection.

Our own death. Our own resurrection. Have we the faith to apply God's words to ourselves, as they should be applied? Have I the hope to realise that it is to me he speaks, as it was to Israel, as it was to Mary, in these words: 'You are all fair, my love … You have ravished my heart' (Sol 4:7,9)? Or again, 'I will betroth you to me for ever; I will betroth you to me in righteousness and in justice, in steadfast love, and in mercy. I will betroth you to me in faithfulness; and you shall know the Lord' (Hos 2:19, 20). Have I the courage to be loved, or am I like the man in the parable of the ten talents, who does nothing with the treasure he has been given? Do I dare hear God say to me: 'You are my beloved daughter'? 'You are my beloved son'?

Mary dared. She heard and did not doubt what God was saying to her. There was no false humility as she cried out, 'Behold, henceforth all generations will call me blessed; for he who is mighty has done great things for me' (Lk 1:48, 49). This is true greatness, the wholehearted acceptance that one is chosen in love for a mighty task. This is surely the queen of the psalms, standing at the right hand of the king, in 'gold of Ophir':

'The princess is decked in her chamber with gold-woven robes;
In many-coloured robes she is led to the king,
With her virgin companions, her escort, in her train.
With joy and gladness they are led along
As they enter the palace of the king' (Ps 45:14-15).

Faith, hope and love may be given to us as gifts, or we may have to win them – because they can be willed. We should not forget that Mary greeted the annunciation with fear: the great act of faith immortalised in the words 'Behold the handmaid of the Lord; let it be to me according to your word' did not spring lightly to her lips – it emerged from a spirit so deeply troubled that is was surely more a plea than an exclamation.

'Endurance produces character, and character produces hope.' When the angel's message is corroborated at the visitation, Mary's faith is rewarded with hope. She finds strength and joy in embracing her destiny. The jubilation of the *Magnificat* rings down the centuries.

She gives birth, freeing creation from bondage to decay. 'Those who live according to the flesh set their minds on the things of the flesh ... to set the mind on the flesh is death, but to set the mind on the Spirit is life and peace' (Rom 8:5-6). How hard it is to free ourselves from that thrall to the immediate, the tangible – to feed the senses and not the soul! How difficult to deliver ourselves from our fears, our concerns, our appetites, our distractions – even though that delivery, painful as the travail of childbirth, will bring new life, new creation: 'We know that the whole creation has been groaning in travail together until now; and not only the creation, but we ourselves, who have the first fruits of the spirit, groan inwardly as we wait for adoption as sons, the redemption of our bodies' (Rom 8:22, 23).

Mary could have said, in the words of Timothy, 'I have fought the good fight, I have finished the race, I have kept the faith' (2 Tim 4:7). Nothing more, and nothing less, is asked of us. If the faith does not come freely to us, we cannot give up. The example is there for us at the very beginning of the Old Testament: Jacob wrestling with God, and declaring between gritted teeth: 'I will not let you go, unless you bless me' (Gen 32:26). It is significant that this is the point where Jacob's name is changed to the name by which his descendents will ever after be known, 'Israel', 'He who strives with God': 'Your name shall no more be called Jacob, but Israel, for you have striven with God and with men, and have prevailed' (Gen 32:28).

Jesus urges the same point when he talks about prayer. Using the example of the man going to his neighbour's house to look for bread, after a friend has arrived unexpectedly, he says: 'I tell you, though he will not get up and give him anything because he is his friend, yet because of his importunity he will rise and give him whatever he needs. And I tell you, ask, and it will be given you; seek, and you will find; knock, and it will be opened to you' (Lk 11:8-10).

If we are not given the gifts of faith, hope and love freely, we have to fight for them. When we have fought that fight, we can confidently expect the crown that Mary received – the crown of righteousness, of glory, of life: 'Henceforth, there is laid up for you the crown of righteousness, which the Lord, the righteous judge, will award me on that Day, and not only to me but upon all who have loved his appearing' (2 Tim 4:8). 'And when the chief Shepherd is manifested you will obtain the unfading crown of glory' (1 Peter 5:4). 'Be faithful until death, and I will give you the crown of life' (Rev 2:10).

Mary goes to her glory, the new Zion, the Ark of the New Covenant:

'Lo, we heard of it in Ephrathah,
we found it in the fields of Ja'ar.
'Let us go to his dwelling place;
let us worship at his footstool!'

Arise, O Lord, and go to thy resting place,
Thou and the ark of thy might.

For the Lord has chosen Zion;
He has desired it for his habitation:
'This is my resting place for ever;
here I will dwell, for I have desired it' (Ps 132: 6-8, 13-14).

Prayer

Mary, in the meditative prayer that is the Rosary, I have travelled with you through the scriptures. In that immense journey, certain images burned themselves into my heart:

I remember Elijah, standing in the mouth of the cave and finding God in the still, small voice.

I remember Ezekiel and his strange vision of the valley of the dry bones: 'and the breath came into them, and they lived, and stood upon their feet, an exceedingly great host'.

I remember David, 'leaping and dancing before the Lord'.

I remember Simeon, reluctantly shouldering his distasteful burden, and discovering that sometimes it is enough just to be in Christ's presence.

I remember Mary and the other women on that Easter Sunday morning, searching for you among dead things.

Above all, I remember Lazarus, and I pray that I might hear the words Christ spoke to him: 'Unbind him, and let him go'.

Afterthought

Console-toi, tu ne me cherchais pas si tu ne m'avais trouvé.
(Be consoled, you would not be seeking me
if you had not found me.)
Pascal, *Pensées*, Section 7, No. 553

Notes

1. David F Wright, *Chosen by God: Mary in Evangelical Perspective* (London, Marshall Pickering, 1989) 123.
2. *Sacrosanctum Consilium: Dogmatic Constitution on the Sacred Liturgy,* article 13.
3. 'As a gospel prayer, centred on the mystery of the redemptive incarnation, the Rosary is ... a prayer with a clearly christological orientation. Its most characteristic element, in fact, the litany-like succession of Hail Marys, becomes in itself an unceasing praise of Christ, who is the ultimate object both of the angel's announcement and of the greeting of the mother of John the Baptist: "Blessed is the fruit of your womb" (Lk 1:42). We would go further and say that the succession of Hail Marys constitutes the warp on which is woven the contemplation of the mysteries'. (*Marialis Cultus*, 46).
4. Without its contemplative element 'the Rosary is a body without a soul, and its recitation is in danger of becoming a mechanical repetition of formulas and of going counter to the warning of Christ: "And in praying do not heap up empty phrases as the Gentiles do; for they think that they will be heard for their many words" (Mt. 6:7). By its nature the recitation of the Rosary calls for a quiet rhythm and a lingering pace, helping the individual to meditate on the mysteries of the Lord's life as seen through the eyes of her who was closest to the Lord. In this way the unfathomable riches of these mysteries are unfolded'. (ibid, 47)
5. Romans 5:3-5.
6. Romano Guardini, 'Form and Meaning of the Rosary Devotion' in *The Rosary of Our Lady,*
7. Genesis 32:26.
8. Konradin Ferrari d'Achieppo, *Der Stern von Bethlehem,* (Berlin, 1994).
9. Inscription from Lapis Venetus, uncovered in Venice in 1674.
10. St Augustine, *Confessions,* bk 10, ch 27.
11. Romans 8:26.
12. P. Teilhard de Chardin, *Towards the Future,* (London: Collins, 1975) 86-87.